cover photo: *Oritapis*, 2D/3D carpet, design: Matali Crasset, 1999
project Glassex, photograph: Lon Van Keulen

editor assistant: Stéphane Argillet

special thanks to

Juliette Soulez, Guillaume Bardet, Thibaut Sailly, Christophe Fillioux, Dominge Dado,
Guy Bouchet, Hervé Ternisien, Thomson Multimédia, Domodinamica,
Dominique Feintrenie, Stephan Pigeyre, Lon Van Keulen, La Manufacture de Sèvres,
Mario Pignata, Guy Bouchet, Vincent Leroux, Morgane Le Gall, Nicolas Profit,
Lexon/Thomson, Markus Richter, Thomson Multimédia, Dominique Feintrenie,
Arnaud Vincent

© ÉDITIONS DIS VOIR, 1999
3, RUE BEAUTREILLIS
75004 PARIS

ISBN 2-906-571-84-9

PRINTED IN EUROPE

BEEF

BRÉTILLOT/VALETTE

MATALI CRASSET

PATRICK JOUIN

JEAN-MARIE MASSAUD

STARCK'S KIDS?

this serie edited by
PIERRE STAUDENMEYER

in the same serie

BOREK SÌPEK
Philippe Louguet, Dagmar Sedlickà

JASPER MORRISON
Charles Arthur Boyer, Federica Zanco

ELIZABETH GAROUSTE & MATTIA BONETTI
Pierre Staudenmeyer, Nadia Croquet, Laurent Le Bon

RON ARAD
Raymond Guidot, Olivier Boissière

ANDREA BRANZI
François Burkhardt, Cristina Morozzi

ROGER TALLON
Gilles de Bure, Chloé Braunstein

BEEF
BRÉTILLOT/VALETTE
MATALI CRASSET
PATRICK JOUIN
JEAN-MARIE MASSAUD

STARCK'S KIDS?

Pascale Cassagnau
Christophe Pillet

CONTENTS

Design in the 90s: subtraction objets

'It seems everybody's trying to find a word that expresses more bigness than the word 'supermodel'... hypermodel... gigamodel... megamodel. Michael suggested that our inability to come up with a word bigger than supermodel reflects our inability to deal with the crushing weight of history we've created for ourselves as a species.' Douglas Coupland, Microserfs.

'The best place to view Los Angeles of the next millennium is from the ruins of its alternative future. Standing on the sturdy cobblestone foundations of the General Assembly Hall of the Socialist City of Llano del Rio—Open Shop Los Angeles' utopian antipode—you can sometimes watch the Space Shuttle in its elegant final descent towards Rogers Dry Lake. Dimly on the horizon are the giant sheds of Air Force Plant 42 where Stealth Bombers (each costing the equivalent of 10,000 public housing units) and other, still top secret, hot rods of the apocalypse are assembled. Closer at hand, across a few miles of creosote and burro bush, and the occasional grove of that astonishing yucca, the Joshua tree, is the advance guard of approaching suburbia, tract homes on point.' Mike Davis, City of Quartz. Excavating the Future in Los Angeles.

'I drank soy milk and ran the metric mile. I had a thing I clipped to the waistband of my running trunks, a device that weighed only

*three and a half ounces and had a readout showing distance traveled
and calories burned and length of stride. I carried my house keys in
an ankle wallet that fastened with a velcro closure. I didn't like to
run with house keys jiggling in my pocket. The ankle wallet answered
a need. It spoke directly to a personal concern. It made me feel there
were people out there in the world of product development and
merchandising and gift cataloguing who understood the nature of my
little nagging needs.'* Don Delillo, *Underworld.*

Science-fiction, in film as in literature, is a reflexive model
through which to view present reality in the form of a story. Design and
its environment-objects also offer a surface for inscription and projection
which social analysis can use as a starting-point for new hypotheses.
Objects seen in the space for which they were intended fulfil a function
of symbolic representation, giving to design the added dimension of
producing fictions for the present.

Science-fiction presupposes an implicit system of referents with
multiple possible meanings. It thus sets up a space of passage in which to
conduct analyses and explore hypotheses. Moreover, the domain of
science-fiction, like that of design, lies on the boundary between public
and private space, and articulates the dual notions of the individual and
the collective, the private and the communal. Issues in both design and
science-fiction are approached from a collective standpoint.

In science-fiction narratives, objects are vectors of communication.
Somewhere between the pure functionality of a utilitarian object and the
decorative dimension of an accessory, science-fiction objects act as
interfaces for communication and the exchange of symbolic values. Part
accessory, part ergonomic prosthesis, these objects are extensions of the
body engaged in action: be they weapons, tools or instruments, they
accompany or serve the inscription of social functions, of a hierarchy. An
object is the vehicle of meanings which define a particular state of affairs.
In George Lucas's film *THX1138,* which shows human society alienated

before a faceless authority, the multitude of objects used underlines a fundamental dis-appropriation. Objects contribute to characterizing and constructing spaces. In Stanley Kubrick's film *2001, A Space Odyssey*, furnishings and technological objects suggest the threat of imminent danger. This fantasy construction is produced by a combination of all the objects and the way they are fitted in to their environment. The 'total décor' creates an effect of de-realisation in an antiseptic space: objects are subordinated to a totality of effect which conditions them.

Philippe Starck's 'scenographies' of objects share with the spaces of science fiction a feeling of strangeness which derives from the de-personalisation of their environment. Like the bionic-looking 'pink phone' in Cronenberg's film *eXistenZ*, the kind of bio-design championed by Starck works through a de-realising setting aside of function in the interests of form. This 'aesthetics of disappearance' signals not any effective absence of matter, but a downgraded notion of function. In Philippe Starck's work the gaze becomes the major function, by displacement of the field of signification. This staging of the gaze gives objects fictive development possibilities because it is the instrument of all projections and identifications. Play is one of the key functions here, since the object is intended to diffuse its seductiveness throughout the social tissue.

The 'stealth design' of discreet objects signals a very specific semiology of the denotative and connotative messages conveyed by objects: their plastic semantics is based on a situation analysis which implies both a singular space-time experience and the integration of all the user's faculties. Both the communication of the project and its production of self-validating signs take place in this interactive semantic perspective.

Philippe Starck's adoption of a bio-design approach corresponds to a weakening of the notion of style, since style involves the relationship between human thought and materials. If bio-design came out of a desire to celebrate the memory of life, however, the move towards 'no-design' involves paying homage to collective memory, as Starck makes clear:

'A few years ago I put forward the concept of no-design: the designer was to withdraw behind the screen of a sort of collective memory. One illustration of this is the Miss Sissi lamp. You couldn't say I designed it. When it appeared it seemed totally reactionary. But a short time later it had become a new point of reference. It has undoubtedly been the world's most imitated and copied lamp.'

Philippe Starck underlines here the paradox of a non-style which ends up becoming a figure, a recognizable sign, in its own right. A personal form of creativity with the smallest desire to develop a style is the one that succeeds best in expressing a collective feeling. The *Sissi* Lamp is an example of a synthesis between the collective and the individual. The object transmits signs, it puts out a discourse about itself and the world. In general, the semantic and communicational functions of the sign are self-promoting. That is the message of Philippe Starck's 'nice' objects: they 'chatter' away, telling us a lot about themselves in the process.

Philippe Starck's 'no-design' experiments and his rejection of all stylistic effects, even if it is ultimately impossible to shut out style altogether, stand in marked contrast to the search for expressivity which characterized designers of the 1980s (Memphis, Sottsass, Garouste et Bonetti, Mariscal, Dubuisson…), and the major role they gave to drawing. Starck's attitude to style prefigures the way in which style has been sidelined by the young designers of the 90s.

On the other hand, Philippe Starck's work on 'immateriality' and the 'disappearance' of function has not been taken up in the same way by 90s designers.

They attach great importance to a literal use of materials and highlight the importance of multi-functionality, leaving form behind as a secondary consideration.

If the 80s produced the idea of 'Immaterials', the 90s have invented operative ways to re-materialise objects.

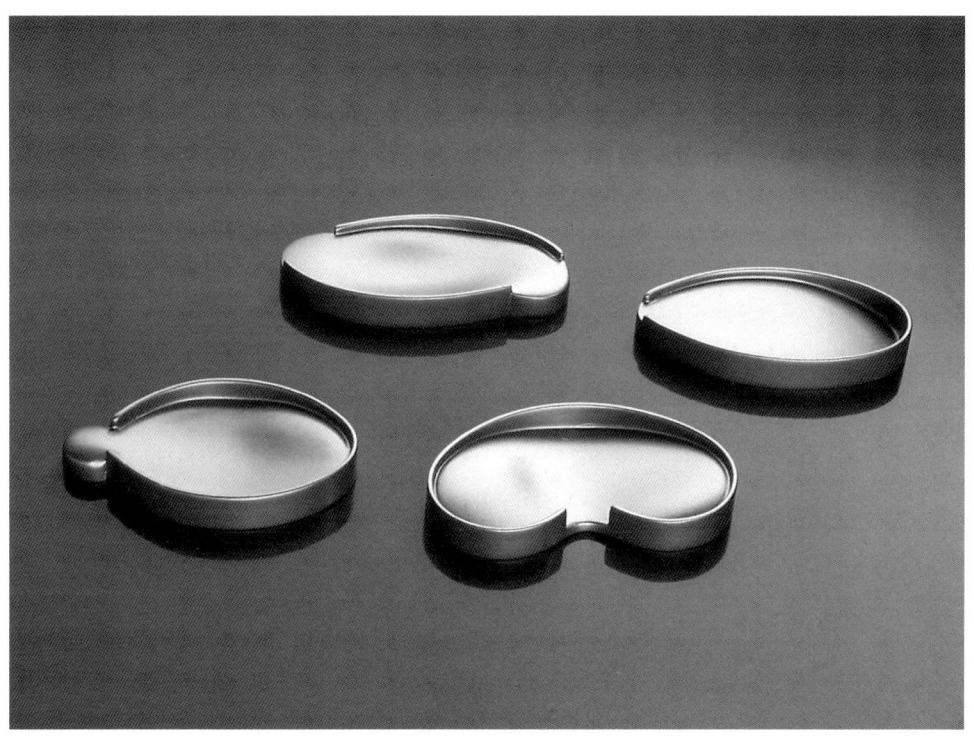

Four ashtrays, 1991
Polished aluminium melting miror 'microbillé'
Design: Brétillot/Valette
Ed: SEITA, France

Ph: Dominge Dado

Transitional forms, and the variable-geometry nature of urban and private spaces, are now generating a nomadic form of design.

Mobility—Movement—Nomadism

At the end of the 90s, fashion, contemporary art and design all seem preoccupied with the recurring themes of mobility, movement, interactivity, user-friendliness and transformational multi- functionality, while the Internet has made virtuality into a cultural reality, a new dimension added to our perception of existing reality. As this new public space, which changes the nature of social relations, continues to develop, mobile technology objects will become increasingly miniaturized to the point where they become interchangeable and multi-functional. The ongoing construction of the virtual space that is the Internet is a symptom of a certain state of the world known as 'globalization', the development of a planetary society. Globalization involves *'a very complex set of multiple networks—economic, associative, cultural, media and migratory—whose most important characteristic is that they are constructed on the basis of a strictly utilitarian rationality, without reference to the sovereignty of states.'*[1]

This global configuration of networked exchange, and the economy of the immaterial which is now taking shape both within the real economy itself and in the ways our image of the world is constructed, are having a major impact on symbol-producing fields such as art, architecture and planning, as well as on the production of objects. Nowadays, looking for answers to the question of how objects should be made involves revisiting notions of use, function and form on the basis of

[1] Bertrand Badie, *Un monde sans souveraineté—Les États entre ruse et responsabilité* (*A World Without Sovereignty: States Trapped between Ruse and Responsibility*), Paris, Fayard,1999. In this substantial essay the author examines the implications of this generalization of exchange for health, human rights, peace, the environment and education, the universal aspirations of mankind.

the new modes of meaning which constitute them. Robotics and artificial intelligence have helped bring about a different definition of service and usage-value, while the spread of computer-assisted creation techniques (graphics packages such as Xpress, Illustrator, Photoshop or design packages like Autocad) emphasizes the 'project culture' and conceptual dimensions of the design process.

The scenarios being developed today in economics, such as the 'Domino Effect' and 'stressed flow' distribution, also mesh with the logic of the global spread of exchange and communication networks, and the accelerating development of technology, which have been gathering pace for several decades now. Artists and architects of the 70s abundantly explored this technological and social flip-side of the contemporary world, producing critiques and action programmes in which technology was mixed with play and anti-functionalism. Thus the Dutch artist Constant's 'New Babylon' situationist project (1969-1974) lays down markers for the re-thinking of contemporary towns and territories.[2] As Chantal Béret emphasizes, '*This different city for a different life is neither a geological city set in a closed landscape, nor a modern, green city; it is a concatenation of networks which stretch endlessly across the territory's space. Their horizontal layering creates the main carrier structure suspended above the surface, which remains free, on huge pillars. Automated factories and trains belong underground, the surface is for people to move around on, while sports grounds, recreational gardens, heliports and (silent) aerodromes are accommodated on raised terraces.*

[2] The whole of this visionary architectural project (models, drawings, texts) was shown last autumn at Witte de With in Rotterdam, in a widely-hailed exhibition called 'New Babylon: the Hyper-Architecture of Desire' (21 November 1998—20 January 1999); see the exhibition catalogue by Mark Wigley: 'Constant's New Babylon: the Hyper-Architecture of desire', Witte de With, Center for Contemporary Art, 0/10 Publishers, Rotterdam, 1998. The Nederlands Architectuurinstituut of Rotterdam recently showed the works of the architect Yona Friedman in an exhibition titled 'Structures serving the Unpredictable' (NAI, 22 May—18 July 1999), which in particular sets in context the architect's manifesto texts on 'Mobile Architecture' and the 'Spatial City'.

There are also hanging 'sectors', sorts of mobile constructions which are continuously being rebuilt in new ways. The most modern experimental construction techniques are used, with electronic calculation of the numerous spatial combinations and new, ultra-lightweight materials such as titanium and nylon, aluminium sheeting and glass.'[3]

The city as imagined by Constant becomes in its turn a place where fictions of self and world can unfold, to produce an aesthetic of everyday life for a hypothetical contemporary subject whose figure is only provisional.

This city territory with its living, service and work zones looks like a utopian world, an exact double of our planetary space. In describing it, the artist-architect and planner has chosen to foreground a certain number of conceptual procedures which are rapidly changing, and a method of analyzing reality which privileges 'situations' over forms.

This theoretical and poetic approach to human geography is contemporaneous with the writings of the art critic Lucy Lippard on the concept of the 'de-materialisation of the art object'. Photography, video, television, all art-forms with neither their own space, nor any material support beyond their intrinsic existence, have helped to change the nature of the work of art, whose main ingredient now is time. Artists, architects and designers now all base their work around a context and procedures of dissemination.

The 1990s have seen the (ludic) redefinition of a black box aesthetics which bears witness to the potency of the communicational paradigm. The Macintosh-designed iMac is a sort of UFO, an object of the third kind, all round and transparent, a technological toy for navigating the Web.

In recent years various demonstration-exhibitions have been organised on the theme of transport, all foregrounding the notion of nomadism. *Propos Mobiles* (Mobile Statements)[4] showed a number of

---

[3] Chantal Béret, Art Press 244 (March 1999), p. 93.
[4] The *Propos Mobiles* exhibition was organized by the Projet 10 association under the aegis of Denis Gaudel.

works of contemporary art for public spaces (François Roche, Franck Scurti, Vito Acconci) which experimented with mobile structures or played with multiple travel metaphors. The American artist has invented a 'packed-up city', a sort of compressed urban landscape that travels around in a 50-metre long caravan. Joep Van Lieshout and Carsten Höller suggest through their mobile structures the possibility of vehicles for experiencing desire and its satisfaction in the form of sensory trips through the city for couples. Numerous examples of mobile structures are found in contemporary creative space, all melding autobiographical fiction with experiments around the themes of travel and territory.

In particular, Andréa Zittel's '*Living units*' (1990) are echoed by the '*Mobile Construction Project for a Training Centre*' in Venice, California, by Lawrence Scarpa and Jennifer Siegel.[5] In the course of a stay in Berlin, Claire Petetin and Philippe Grégoire had the idea of offering the Rollheimer people a new-style gypsy caravan for the 21st century, a nomadic habitat which would be extensible or contractible, an autonomous, recyclable module which can be plugged in like a household electrical item. The project lands in the city as on a carpet and then moves into patches of unused land. In the same spirit, the designer Constantin Grcic has invented a mobile lamp consisting of a light cone in white polypropylene with a wire that can be placed or fixed anywhere.

Mobile Bodies sought to bring out the relations which link objects to their physical and social environment in the late 90s, through the theme of mobility, now that '*the increasing pace of life, changing relationships with space and the city, and social change are forcing us to rethink the everyday objects around us, imagine them in relation to a world in constant movement, and adapt them to new actions and bodies that occupy space differently. French design has already made considerable strides in this direction. Many creators are working to imagine objects able*

[5] On this topic, see 'Mobility design', Axis n° 5/6 (May-June 1999).

Mirors on stands, 1998
miror et stainless steel
Design: Bretillot/Valette
Ed: Guillaume Saalburg Techniques Transparentes

Ph: Guy Bouchet

to keep up with the development of mankind's modes of living by taking on board the theme of mobility.'[6]

For its part, *Mobile*, a lifestyle magazine edited by Chloé Braustein and Olivier Peyricot, presents itself as *'a junction box, a toolbox containing a set of proposals for unsuspected mechanical applications', aiming to explain 'a global vision constructed from local methods of working at lifestyle invention. A lifestyle is a set of complex, protean expressions at the intersection point of a wide range of disciplines (architecture, design, writing, fashion, economics, geography, the plastic arts, the sciences…)'.*

Thus the magazine's various columns bring out the constant interconnections between different cultural registers arranged in flux which organise our concept of reality into sedimented layers, like hypertext.

Mobile structures generate hybrid and composite configurations which parallel the ways in which we think about multiple displacements. The Iranian fashion designer Hussein Chalayan recently created a set of hybrid clothes, both dresses and chairs at the same time, which he calls *Geotropics*. These hybrid structures, half-way between objects and clothes, are part of an experiment in nomadism and bodily mobility. Hussein Chalayan describes the components of Geotropics as follows: *'the idea was to choose a road on a map and look at the countries it crossed, and observe those regions of the world which, like the USA, generate different ways of operating and types of behaviour. I was very*

---

[6] Organized by the Doc Design association, Mobile Bodies (Des Corps Mobiles) brought together the following designers: Pascal Bauer, David Becker, Christian Biecher, Ronan Bouroullec, Matali Crasset, Créa Créa, Thibeau Desombre, Adrien Gardère, Martine Harlé, Patrick Jouin, Thomas Klug, Séverine Lefort, Jean-Marie Massaud, Dominique Mathieu, Bernard Moïse, Olivier Peyricot, Poisson d'Avril, Pothelet and Messager, Frédéric Rieffel, Eric Robin, Frédéric Ruyant, Milan Simic, Roël Stassart, Philippe Teste, Renaud Thiry, Michel Tortel, Alexis Tricoire, Nicolas Trüb. The VIA also organised an exhibition called 'Nomadic Furniture for the 'Passport' Generation' ('Mobiliers nomades pour générations 'passeport') (September-November 1998).

interested in the notion of cultural change over distance.[7] Hussein Chalayan's invention of the 'dress-chair' and Yoshji Yamamoto's creation of an inflatable dress (as seen at his latest show) bring a new dimension to clothing. The stylists Marithé and François Girbaud invented some thirty years ago the concept of 'living in your bag', which involves creating clothes which are also living spaces. The Italian firm Mandarina Duck has re-thought nomadic clothing by creating a rucksack built in to a jacket.

These experiments all set clothing in a wider context, at the interface between the body in movement and three-dimensional space.

Bless's chair clothes, which lie on the border between clothing and furniture accessories, and Dirk Van Saene's 100% paper Throwaway Dress, in particular, offer programmatic examples of possible networking between the new materials technologies industry and the invention of wearable structures.[8]

Equally, experiments by the British designers Anthony Dunne and Fiona Raby are designed to bring out the interaction between objects, electromagnetic environments, electronic products and the body. *'Hertzian Tales'* and *'The Affection Thief'* are object-situations, analysis-interfaces for reality, as well as alternative scenarios for re-conceptualising the interaction between objects and the human subject. The series *'20 Objects For Inhabiting Hertzian Space'* presents phantom objects which people our everyday environment, by creating soundscapes criss-crossed by invisible emanations—hertzian waves. The designers imagine paranoid scenarios relating to the resulting control, power and protection strategies. Answering machines, personal computers, faxes and printers in particular give off radiation which propagates through space. Counter-strategies can be developed to limit this radiation by using protective prosthetic devices.

---

[7] Hussein Chalayan, Beaux Arts Magazine n° 178 (March 1999), p. 46.
[8] A supplement on fashion in the French newspaper Libération lists recent creations combining hybridisation, composite structures and new materials to re-think today's clothing by transforming it into a virtual accessory for showing off or protecting the body (Libération, 10 March 1999).

Representations—Hypotheses about Reality

The Archilab international exhibition of contemporary architecture directed by Marie-Ange Brayer and Frédéric Migayrou places particular emphasis on the links between contemporary modes of transport, technological modes of representation (3-D, computer graphics and CAD software), and our physical experience of constructed space. This tight interweaving of geopolitical and topological levels primarily concerns architecture and planning, which are both reflecting prisms of a particular spatio-temporal situation, and experimental laboratories for the formulation of working hypotheses. From this standpoint, the inscription of time has been shown to play a crucial role in structuring spaces and territories, as Alain Guiheux stresses in connection with the notion of the 'site': *Situational urban planning does not imply some pre-existing formal theory, but rather certain actions and procedures which correspond to the presence of time in the project and as a result of which the purpose and value of the site changes.*[9] Design also contributes to defining a geo-economic space-time by raising the issue of objects.

The exhibition of 30 architect's projects at 'Archilab' gives a good overview of current thinking about the complex links between the process of inventing space and its consequent modes of representation, mediated by constant negotiations. As Frédéric Migayrou reminds us: *When the car first appeared on the scene the psychology of transport changed, along with the space/time relationship, and therefore our relationship to everyday space. The school of thought for which architecture must be based on plans is dying out. There are no longer any pure, empty spaces, they are all complex and coded. In order to make your own mark in them, you have to proceed by assemblage within that complex system. Flexibility, which twenty years ago was an unattainable*

[9] Alain Guiheux, 'Architectures-action', Parpaings n° 2 (April 1999), p. 22.

ideal, is now perfectly possible. Algeco is everywhere, and mobility means being able to move partitions at will.'[10]

The framework of contemporary architecture determines the possibility of a nomadic lifestyle and the creation of a genuine cross-over between different fields of thought and physical spaces. The complex relations which exist between the geo-socio-political conditions of architecture and the ways we imagine our lived environment produce not some exemplary goal, but a process of ongoing invention of the everyday.

The field of contemporary art is also criss-crossed by different hypotheses about reality. A brief survey of the family tree of contemporary art can put into perspective the different thematic domains into which it falls.

'Contemporary art is an ecology of the mind and the senses; an urban, interstitial practice which examines, case by case, the relationships which link us in to our visual and cultural environment. Beyond its reflexive status, this practice also involves providing capital goods for the thought process. Previous art used to capture our attention at a limited point in space-time; current art aims to generate forms of behaviour, making our gaze's many frames sweep across things and producing blocks of time that we can manipulate.'[11]

In his writings on art and in the proposals he puts forward through his exhibitions, the art critic Nicolas Bourriaud situates the scope of contemporary art in terms of interactions and networks. In defining what he calls a 'relational aesthetic', he shows that, in contra-distinction to 70s artists, artists of the 90s work on scale models of communicational situations. Whereas in the 70s *'attitudes were turned into forms'*,[12] today's behavioural art perhaps engenders more social links and shared time.

[10] Frédéric Migayrou, in Beaux-Arts Magazine n° 179 (April 1999), p. 70.

[11] Nicolas Bourriaud, Carsten Höller—*Rosemarie Trockel catalogue*, Musée d'Art Moderne de la Ville de Paris, 1999, p. 66.

[12] 'When Attitudes Turned into Forms' is the title of a programmatic exhibition held in 1969 at the Bern Kunsthalle by Harald Szeemann. This manifesto-exhibition contained a substantial set of works by the neo-Dada Fluxus movement, the post-minimalist movement and Arte Povera.

When he writes here of contemporary artistic practice 'providing capital goods for the thought process', he is echoing Matali Crasset's wish that design should 'put thinking back on centre stage'. If contemporary art is creating a multitude of scenarios based on a 'relational aesthetics', that same dimension can also be seen in the modes of organisation of work which, in the 90s, govern relations between industry and designers. In describing their way of working with industry, Matali Crasset and Jean-Marie Massaud in particular stress issues of organisation and configuration of communication links and human relations, as if the logic of rupture and deliberate misappropriation that characterized the 80s no longer obtained.

In parallel with the constitution of a community-based space and time-frame, contemporary art is generating a multitude of fictions based on imaginary networks. The key element here is the language of information technology.

Sowana, a practitioner of the art of conversation and argument, is actually an artificial artist who has been active on the Internet since 1997. He is a directed dialogue automaton with a natural language interface. Sowana's knowledge-base improves by self-learning as his dialogues develop. He was designed by the Cercle Ramo Nash (alias the artists Paul et Joon Ja Devautour) as part of their 'Artistic Intelligence' virtual project. The hardware that supports this fictitious communication with the artificial character Sowana consists of a 'black box' and a set of iMacs. The subtraction object that is the black box is an example of the virtual and interactive currents flowing through contemporary art and design. The black box aesthetic illustrates the way contemporary work is being 'contaminated' by information and communication technologies. This return to the notion of the black box is taking place on a metaphorical level, with the black box reflecting the world and the social sphere.

In the same way, the artist Sloan Leblanc is making the Linux operating system the subject of his installations which dramatize the world of IT and office systems. Linux, which allows free access to programs and the option of changing them, represents a sort of utopia of personal communication in a networked age. The choice of Linux determines the way the computer operates, from the user interface to peripherals drivers. Sloan Leblanc invites the viewer to become an active agent in a communications bureau called *Tableau de bord* (Control Panel), consisting of two computer workstations with office desks and managers' chairs. The major aesthetic attributes to emerge from this type of environment, strongly influenced by references to science-fiction films, are comfort, ergonomics and functionality. The digital fiction which it creates suggests a user-friendly, community-based conception of IT.

The fictions invented by contemporary art, cinema or fashion constitute a reflexive black box which tells us about the technological and social fictions at work within late 20th-century reality. Hypertext and communication are major features of these fictions, their very representational space and architecture of meaning. Digitally-networked space, and the virtuality and interactivity which flow from it, are generating the new narrative modes and ephemeral temporality of contemporary creation, as well as bringing to it a collective dimension. The hugely expanding private use of the Internet, a world-wide network of interconnected computers, can in some circumstances be reversed to yield possibilities for collective creation. In his catalogue text for the *Cities on the move 2* exhibition, Hans-Ulrich Obrist presents an urban planning project called *Mirage City*, designed by the Japanese architect Arata Izozaki for the suburbs of Hong Kong. His idea is to give the project an interactive, global dimension by inviting architects and the public all over the world to contribute to a Website devoted to Mirage City. For Izozaki, this project avoids the three essentials of modern architecture: territory, boundaries and the vanishing point, in order to produce a new interweaving of space and time. While some sites offer a showcase for fictitious communities, such as Alphaworld (a virtual community of

Justine, chair, 1998
lacquered pipe and oilcloth
Design: Bretillot/Valette
Réalisée pour l'exposition "Justine 'tit' chaise", janvier 1998, Paris
Ph: Hervé Ternisien

graphic designers who have invented their own city), others are concerned with exploring imaginary geographies. Valéry Grancher, for instance, has developed a project called *Self* where web-surfers are invited to leave a message on the Internet in exchange for a real-time image of the Atlantic Ocean or Mount Everest. This online work gradually builds up a collective memory and documentation of an event in process of unfolding, by progressive enrichment of its data over time.

The emergence of the Internet and the Web in the late 80s has helped to redefine notions of public space, identity and citizenship. Indeed, the Internet has created a new territory, which is superimposed on terrestrial territory without negating it, whose specificity is to engender a public, world-wide space-time with political and legal ramifications. The cyber-space of the Web doubles up the real world, running in parallel and in constant negotiation with it. Like the public spaces created by cities or the media, the Web is a space for the inscription of signs and cultural, political and social values, as well as the locus of the conditions of possibility of their conversion between domains (private-public, singular-collective, internal-external, natural-cultural)—a conversion which takes place in a virtual, interactive mode.

In this new space the nature of citizenship and identity is redefined, in particular through discussion groups which produce an art of conversation where, paradoxically, communicating subjects can be totally ignorant of the identity of their Internet interlocutors and their location in the world. The invention of 'avatars' is symptomatic of the ghostly nature of the Internet, and these cyber-phantoms are its absolute quintessence, like the Japanese 'Kyoko Dates' who exchange information and data without ever revealing their sexual or social identity. These new ghosts are genuine doubles, neither true nor false but simply plausible. The anonymity of net-surfing subjects brings a virtual dimension to the exchange regime, while the possible and the probable, the current and the non-current, produce a multitude of different temporal sequences and ways of communicating.

The creative field of design, like contemporary art or fashion, finds itself today at the interface between cyber-space and the world of mass-produced objects, between the future-fictions of the Internet and new technologies, and new modes of economic production of objects and signs. Now more than ever, creating objects (whether in an industrial or experimental design context) carries political and aesthetic implications for the inscription of cultural and economic signs into the real world.

As in the fields of artificial intelligence and robotics, where hypotheses about the mechanization of living beings are constructed with a view to inventing procedures for learning or for the optimization of adaptive knowledge, the function of design objects today may be one of analysis, and to invent scenarios which will promote new ways of thinking about. In view of the rapid spread of video games, tamagotchi, automatic household appliances, and shape-memory synthetic materials, in the age of stressed flow economics, the 'work' of design probably consists in 'explaining', through the creation of objects, the social and aesthetic implications of these new technologies and the consequences of their use. The object does not need to justify or illustrate the invention of a technique or the establishment of an economic system, its role is rather to accompany their use, and perhaps then propose that it is time to stand back from them or even leave them behind altogether.

Style

In this context, certain notions central to the field of design, such as function, use, style, comfort, and others more peripheral (mobility, inter-activity, environment) which are constituted in the course of constant negotiation, can be seen today as spaces of meaning in need of reconfiguration.

One of the recurrent features of 90s design is the sidelining of style. Style is one of the fundamental categories in the history of art and design, functioning as an operative concept for the listing and classification of historical objects. In his canonical essay '*Stilfragen—Questions of Style. A History of Ornamentation*' (1893), Aloïs Riegl defined style as an artistic intention whose symbolic function was to circumvent chaos and fill the void.

According to traditional sense of the term, style plays a prescriptive role in the design of an object, as well as serving to classify it coherently in relation to a set of codes. When defined in this way as a collective attribute, style contributes to a process of generalization and integration. If on the other hand a particular style should transgress the system to which it belongs, then it implies on the contrary a process of individuation.

According to the contemporary theory of style, which treats it as a part of communication theory, style involves paradoxical play with a code system.

If modern design, which developed out of the Bauhaus aesthetic, led to the emergence of a strong style like that found in modernist architecture, it was because of a process of over-coding: functionalism was a style that deliberately set itself apart from prevailing ideological and aesthetic norms. Standardization through rationalization as a means to solve the problems of democracy and social relations was the political aesthetic of modernity.

In the course of the 90s we have seen the replacement of standardized objects by interactive ones which have a different way of fitting into their ecosystems. Notions such as fractal subjects, environment, and the dispersion of criteria, correspond to different modalities of meaning, rooted in complexity, fragmentation, citation and hybridization. The shift from the consumer to the communication society brought about by the emergence of information, telematic and audio-visual technologies, affects political and cultural decision-making processes. The whole cultural market-place is governed by the over-arching network-system, so giving priority to images and signs. 90s design seems to be broadly characterized by a desire to operate outside the binary logic of style. Rejecting style as both collective expression and individual vision, designers of the 90s are trying to rethink the question of objects from a standpoint which puts considerations of style to one side. The works of Constantin Grcic and Marteen Van Severen are examples of this deliberate weakening of style. The purpose of 'breaking out' of the style dialectic in this way is to make it possible for the object to appeal in a personal way to people of average tastes. The insistence of young French designers on only looking towards industry should be seen in the light of this search for a 'neutral' quality in objects or works designed to reach a wide public. For Patrick Join in particular, the aim of industrial design is to create discreet, well-behaved objects whose self-effacing nature is in inverse proportion to their mass-audience distribution. Objects with this quality of anonymity irrigate the social sphere all the more effectively for being secret.

That is why the Dutch designers' collective Droog design proclaims the principle of the non-expressivity of objects, their lack of all affects. Objects like '*Ray Chair*' or '*Paper Cupboard*' exemplify this search for a provisional form of expression through a DIY aesthetics, because they express a discredited state of consumption and progress. Their rejection of the register of efficient forms, and use of 'poor' or misappropriated materials, offer a telling image of entropy.

The adjective 'Droog' calls to mind the definition of the 'neutral' ('le neutre') that Roland Barthes gives in *Le Degré zéro de l'écriture*: '*neutral writing in fact rediscovers the primary condition of classical art: instrumentality. But this time, form as an instrument is no longer at the service of a triumphant ideology; it is the mode of a new situation of the writer, the way a certain silence has of existing; it deliberately foregoes any elegance or ornament, for these two dimensions would reintroduce Time into writing, and this is a derivative power which contains History.*'[13]

The disappointing aspect of the objects produced by Droog Design is a deliberate move in the search for new ways of giving exposure to

[13] Roland Barthes, *Le Degré zéro de l'écriture*, Paris, Seuil, 1972, pp. 56-7; translated as *The Zero Degree of Writing* by Annette Lavers and Colin Smith, London, Cape, 1984, pp. 61-2.

projects, rather than trying to present objects that are particularly attractive.

This quest for total impassivity and impersonality, excluding even the slightest residual effect of style such as is found in functionalism, is clearly expressed in the 'Stealing Beauty, British Design Now' exhibition at the ICA in London.[14] The various installations are the work of young British designers working directly in the spirit of the principles expounded by the Droog Design designers at the Rotterdam Kunsthalle in 1998.

Their experiments involve introducing slight differences into objects without qualities.

The London exhibition contains a set of experiments which are not structural, but rather represent the expression of an urgency, a necessary precarity; the various objects, furniture-situations and clothes all develop futuristic scenarios which explore the future as a drift towards ruin. As in the stories of Philip K. Dick, the works of the young British designers suggest ruined objects from the 'day after', with their attempt at a residual, late 20th-century form of communication.

'The toaster had dissolved sometime during the day and reformed itself as a rubbishy, quaint, nonautomatic model. Not even pop-up, he discovered as he poked bleakly at it. The refrigerator that greeted him was an enormous belt-driven model, a relic that had floated into being from god knew what distant past; it was even more obsolete than the turret-top G.E. shown in the TV commercial (...) The form TV set had been a template imposed as successor to other templates, like the procession of frames in a movie sequence. Prior forms, he reflected, must carry on an invisible, residual life in every object. The past is latent, is submerged, but still there, capable of rising to the surface once the later imprinting unfortunately—and against ordinary

[14] 'Stealing Beauty: British Design Now', ICA, London, 3 April-23 May 1999. The exhibition included works by: Azumi, Michael Anastassiades, Ann-Sophie Back, Georg Baldele, Torn Boontje, Rebecca Brown, British Creative Decay, Anthony Dunne and Fiona Raby, El ultimo grupo, FAT, Mike Health, Michael Marriot, Muf, The Light Surgeons.

experience—vanished. The man contains—not the boy—but earlier men, he thought. History began a long time ago.'[15] *Ubik* is a futuristic story, written in paradoxical tenses, which reverses the direction of time: the characters are condemned to re-experience time, moving back from the future to the past. In this respect, Philip K. Dick attaches great importance to the fate of objects which are the bearers of the keys to human time and memory.

The rejection of all stylistic effect, the sidelining of the designer's identity: Bump, FAT, British Creative Decay, 6876 all present themselves as anonymous collectives and, like the American artists who make up the Bureau of Inverse Technology (BIT), they bear witness to a precise aim, rather than the post-modern urge merely to level values. Above all, by developing a corpus of fictions rather than making objects, English designers are imagining scenarios of the future in the present, inverting the generally-accepted perspective of science-fiction. What we see here are political-fiction scenarios rather than any production of intelligent or 'smart' objects.

Attitude—Objets—Environment—Ecosystem

Looking at contemporary design and late 20th-century architecture, we can detect in the objects they invent a set of attitudes, behaviour patterns and ways of thinking which reveal a close attentiveness to the ecosystem. Thus the experimental designs by the Dutch MVRDV architecture group (Windy Maas, Jacob van Rijs, Nathalie de Vries) for the Dutch pavilion at the forthcoming Expo 2000 in Hanover offer a façade-less architecture composed of 7 landscapes piled on top of each other, running from the natural to the high-tech.[16] The architect-designers have invented an architectural utopia which describes the conditions of

[15] Philip K. Dick, *Ubik*, Panther Science Fiction, 1973, pp. 118-119.
[16] The MVRDV 'Dutch Pavilion Expo 2000 in Hanover' was on display at the Nederlands Architectuurinstituut in Rotterdam in April-May 1999.

Untiltled, basket, 1992
cladding of galuchat and aluminium
Design: Bretillot/Valette
Ed: Product File International, Angleterre

Ph: Christophe Fillioux

Matali Crasset's logotype, 1994

Beef's logotype

possibility of building in a restricted territory—the Netherlands being the most densely-populated country on Earth—by proposing more economical uses of water and open spaces. This project redefines landscape design by offering efficient management of space on a vertical axis, which is paradoxical in the country of polders and an otherwise purely horizontal definition of territory. The MVRDV '*Metacity/-Datatown*' project involves translating the quantitative variables of an urban environment into computer-generated images, by inventing working hypotheses based on statistics collected in order to help to work out a new configuration of green spaces. The game program invented by Kas Oosterhuis for the Reitdiep garden city in the Netherlands makes use of all the parameters that go into the design of a city. '*Attractor game*' is a game of 'attractions' in which players manage the economy of this city which, like a sponge, soaks up and expels materials, people, information and data, like the migratory birds which come and go in its space. Designed for non-experts (in fact, for the city's future inhabitants), the game displays the various ecological levels—those of both natural and socio-political ecology—that make up the city: '*In physical terms we are all subject to the same 'common denominators' such as quarks, the planets, ideas, language, programs, the speed of light. We are all part of a vast information flow; we ourselves are information and we swim in a sea of data. According to one definition, life is the ability to direct the flow of information. (...) (In the city), the ecological balance includes people entering and leaving, as well as imported and exported data, information coming in, staying around, then leaving again.*'[17]

　　　The Roche DSV & Sie architects' collective has been working for some years on an ecological project (in the political sense of the word) looking at the many different contexts of architecture. For their *Soweto Memorial Museum* (1997) the architects worked with the political and geographical realities of the site in order gradually to bring forth out of the ground a

---

[17] Kas Oosterhuis, in *Archilab catalogue*, Edition Ville d'Orléans, 1999, p. 186.

memorial that would give full recognition to those realities. The natural environment anchors the architecture by acting as a situation-revealer. The architecture is built up step by step rather than imposed in one go.

Writing of the context in which images are invented and realised in western art, the art historian Ernst Gombrich referred to an 'ecology of images' which stresses the importance of place (place of origin, destination). The architectural projects of the François Roche DSV & Sie agency are constructing a poetics of political ecology (in the sense of the ways in which we inhabit the world and its forms).

The type of ecosystem configuration that has become widespread at the end of the 20th century implies a horizontal-matrix economic and social organisation which marks a break with the previous vertical mode of exchange. However, this environmental configuration was already a leitmotif of design as early as the 1960s. For Roger Tallon in particular, design constructed a set of relations between all the elements that went to make up an environment. Objects are ordered within systems that evolve with time, their function being to communicate with their users. The modes of reception of projects which transform the users into true interlocutors, and the fact that economic and commercial processes are take into account at the design stage, give Roger Tallon's productions a real interactive dimension. The syntagmatic nature of his conception of form and function was confirmed in 1969 when he wrote: '*Form does not flow from the analysis of one function but from the analysis of all functions.*'

In the 90s, the informational paradigm has come to act as an economic and stock-control model within the overall framework of an information economy.

The production system of 90s design projects, their modes of conception and 'soft' modelling methods, attest the potency of the 'horizontal' informational model in the philosophy of projects. Project conception processes, torn between simulation and model-making, are coming closer and closer to an economy of relations and exchanges of the so-called 'stressed flow' type. Continuous experimentation and data interaction leads to the construction of complete systems. The concatenation of procedures has sidelined the logic of breaking with the past and displaced the loss of the referent towards a loss of the original. The ecosystem of objects in the 90s has led to an era in which the media and the flow of information are creating an 'ecological niche' for images and signs.

Language—The Future-Fiction of the Object— Communicating the Project

For some years already, Matali Crasset's work has involved inventing playful objects for nomadic lifestyles, objects whose main quality is to displace their reading codes. The notion of 'mobile bodies' operates here on two levels: objects are put together according to a combinational logic, but they also create amusing linguistic puzzles. Matali Crasset's objective is to set forms and typologies in motion. If the 1980s invented an aesthetic of mobile objects in the primary sense of the term, through a rhetoric of foldability and things on wheels, the late 90s are more concerned with thinking about how to renew uses and functions, and how to make unusual use of materials by decontextualising them.

The street furniture project named 'Empathic chair', with its six 'Extensions', consists in a series of adjustable chairs made from recycled plastic, designed 'to spread generosity around town'. The chairs proclaim their own anonymity, but also emphasize their ability to generate immediate, spontaneous and non-hierarchical new uses: looking at the sky, protecting birds, watching over children, listening to the wind, securing a bike, having lunch.

Revisiting cinema historian François Dalbéra's operative metaphor for cinematic space about the 'fable' and the 'material', it is clear that in

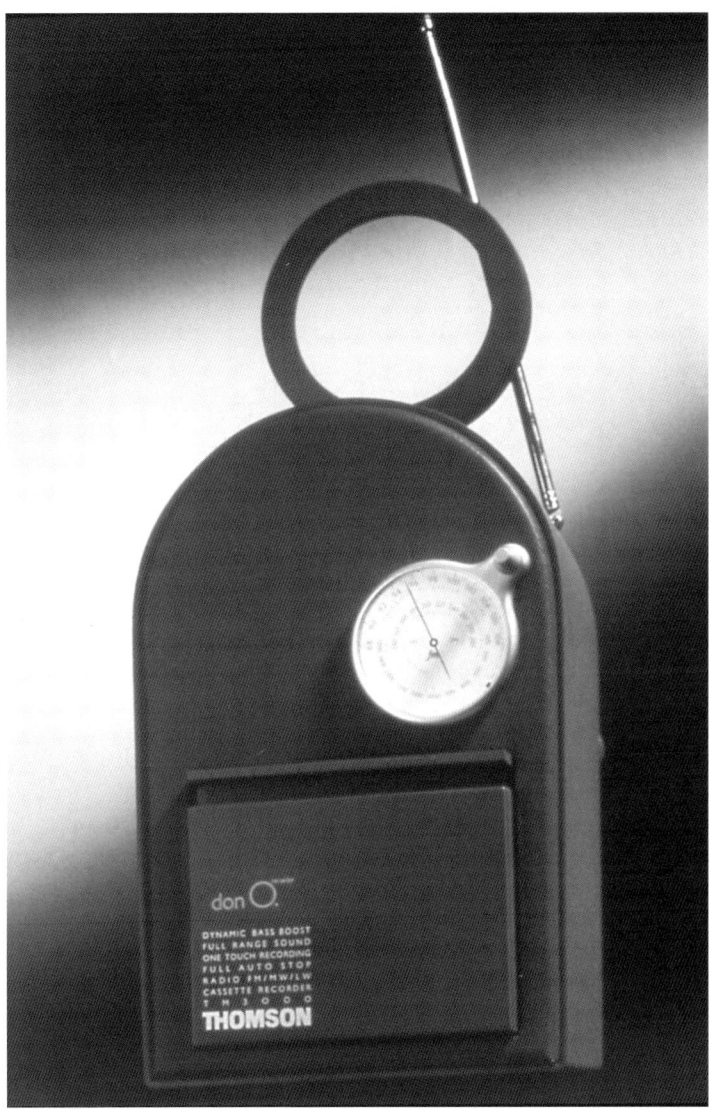

Don O, portable radio-tape player, 1995
plastic ABS
Design: Matali Crasset
Art director: Philippe Starck

Ed & Ph: Thomson Multimédia

Matali Crasset's work the material is relegated to the background in favour of the fable. The different types of plastic used initiate reflection on the many different possible uses, and micro-fictions (narrative fragments) convey those various forms and uses and organise the 'programme'. One characteristic of Matali Crasset's work is the way objects are modelled in words and drawings. *'Quand Jim monte à Paris'* ('When Jim Goes to Paris'), *'Marie a ses petites manies'* ('Marie has her Little Quirks'), *'Jules is dandy'* are narrative as much as usage programmes. Their titles provide keys for reading the objects and understanding their function; the words bring about a process of crystallization which underlines the visual information and helps in its identification. The tense regime (pure present indicative) of these narrative propositions, and their syntactic structure, which points to the beginnings of a plot, both hold up a mirror to the diverse and random possible uses that might be suggested by multi-functional furniture. *'Quand Jim monte à Paris'* is a folding bed for two people which can be stored vertically in a spare column from which bedside accessories (lamp, alarm clock) are hung. *'Jules is dandy'* tells us in a negative way about a character with no identity, through a dual-function object which is both a chair and a storage space. Matali Crasset's work comes down to creating objects and dramatising spaces by inventing 'a range of mobile, multi-functional objects which can transform in line with our wishes and become defined on contact with people, so that they are situated by use.'

Others of her creations are simultaneously items of furniture and environment-spaces, such as *'Théo de 2 à 3'* ('Theo from 2 to 3'), a stool which converts into a siesta mattress, or *'Work at hôm'*. *'Quand Jim monte à Paris'* exemplifies the idea of an *'intimate cocoon extended to friends, who are not merely offered a spare bed, but an individual space complete with a lighting system and clock which turn into a bedside lamp and an alarm.'*

If the functions of generosity and conviviality are much to the fore here, humour and language games are the driving influence behind the little technological objects created for Thomson Multimédia. Words 'open up' and direct their meaning: thus *Icipari* ('Paris Calling') is a simple loudspeaker whose name sums up literally and humorously its sound-diffusing function. *Don O* is a radio-cassette player organised around the idea of sound of different frequencies diffusing in circular patterns, a fact which also dictates its ergonomics. The primary interactive dimension which is a feature of this type of object is supplemented here by an invitation to play with it in a fresh and individually imaginative way. *Music in a bag* is a rucksack with built-in listening facilities, which leaves the hands free.

The language function is also important for communication, which is a key issue for designers of the 90s generation. Communicating the project is now the primary objective of the work of designers such as Matali Crasset. The logo which she has invented as a professional avatar works as a recognition signal, an identificatory trademark.

By inventing a humorous-sounding code-name for themselves—*R*echerche, *A*utoproduction, *D*esign *I*ndustriel ('Experimentation, Self-Production, Industrial Design')—the RADIs have managed to generate a communication and self-promotion phenomenon around their work. In this case, language is 'installing' into reality a programme (industrial design) designated as such, in the same way that record labels derive their image strength from the verbal inventiveness of their names (*Hydrogen, Distance, Dukebox…*). The invention of independent labels in the music field comes from a desire to rival the large commercial publishers and pirate their commercial logic. The verbal inventiveness of their acronyms gives groups an individual linguistic identity while maintaining the anonymity of members of their musical community. The collective art of the flyer and the increasingly widespread use of logos and acronyms signify a rejection of style and the individual signature.

Since the end of the 80s, the contemporary art scene has itself seen the 'disappearance' of individual names: the Ozone Group, I. F. P.

(Information, Fiction, Publicité), Stream TV, Greyworld, all assert that they have sidelined artistic identity in order to bring out the collective, anonymous aspect of contemporary work.

Internet sites like *Mediaboy, Jodi, Supermad* and *Simulator* cultivate an undifferentiated style of expression, pursuing the kind of 'disappearance' aesthetic which conceptual artists like Ian Wilson had already used in the 1970s on the basis of their analysis of television. These attitudes reveal a questioning of the notion of author and the economy of the work that derives from it.

Multi-Functionality—Mobility

The nomadic function of present-day objects reveals an underlying nomadism of domestic spaces which are awaiting redefinition. Corresponding to the multiple uses of everyday spaces is a relocation of objects and furniture inside the home. While a dual process of privatization of public space and 'publicisation' of private space has been underway for several decades now, the identities of specialized spaces in the home and the workplace (bedroom, kitchen, office, living room) have been losing their autonomy and specificity. The two spheres of work and private life are more and more losing their separateness as teleworking techniques develop. Equally, objects and items of furniture are constantly changing their identities, shifting between being main modules and accessories. The fact that present-day objects are becoming nomadic fits them to become parts of combinatory structures. Designed with the aid of a 'Carte Blanche' scholarship from the VIA, Matali Crasset's *'Work at home'* is a home office unit comprising a fixed arch of storage compartments and a mobile multimedia unit intended for teleworking. As a communication object, *'Work at home'* lies somewhere between a workstation, a convivial space and a laboratory. The furniture itself has two modes of occupying space and two states: depending on the state of activity or rest, the modules themselves extend or retract. This sort of computerised toolbox which has moved into domestic space signals new ways of working from home, dependent on a privatization of public space and a 'publicisation' of private. Matali Crasset gives a humorous description of possible changes to the domestic sphere: *'At home you will be able to tap away on your keyboard while making a toasted sandwich.'*

At the last Furniture Fair (January 1999), the VIA had an exhibition on the theme of 'multimedia comfort', based on the three fundamentals of multimedia: pictures, sound, and the resulting composite space. A certain number of today's designers are actually rethinking furniture units in the light of the new and dominant position which image and media technologies now occupy in the household.

In an essay on 20th-century architectural theory, Beatriz Colomina analyses the formation of private space in the midst of public space, and the way in which architecture is 'produced' by the media, explaining that *'the present-day home has become a media centre, which will change forever our understanding of both the public and the private.'*[18] The ever-growing role of the Internet in both public and private space, as seen in the use of email, discussion groups and online services, transforms our living and working places into spaces for private creation (our individual appropriation of computerised tools) and public communication (our participation in collective dialogue).

In the present-day home, any room in a private dwelling can become by turns a place to work, rest or link up with the outside world, each of which implies a different arrangement for the body. On the other hand, workplaces which are turning more and more into telecommunication spaces, can be transformed by tele-technologies into convivial spaces or auditoria. Designed by the Zébulon ('Zebedee') agency, the *'Chill-out' platform* is a jigsaw puzzle which by turns can become a small living room, an intimate space for a couple to watch television, or a day-bed for

[18] Beatriz Colomina, *La publicité du privé*, Editions HXY, p. 167.

relaxation. '*Duchesse brisée*' ('Broken Duchesse'), by Alfredo Häberli and Christophe Marchand, takes the form of a sofa-bath whose composite structure allows the adoption of any position, according to whether one is working, eating or 'wallowing' at a moment of relaxation. Jérôme Gauthier's '*Trait d'union*' ('Hyphen') project, designed under the ægis of the VIA's ongoing competition scheme, consists of a set of collective furniture which nevertheless leaves open the possibility of the space's appropriation by an individual user. '*Trait d'union*' contains a set of three base modules, one seat and two poufs, which can be combined in any order to fit the possible situations of social conviviality that might arise: 'because our living spaces are the theatres of many different activities, the multiplicity of individual forms of behaviour requires the adaptable provision of collective comfort.'[19]

On occasion, the theme of nomadic, multi-functional furniture can be exploited in a literal way by designers who 'dramatize' possible mobile statements.

Olivier Peyricot, for example, has designed *Bubble*, a nomadic seating system of 3, 6, and 9 inflatable balloons held together by a lycra envelope; when not in use, the units pack away into a small box. Renaud Thiry, who works under the Flandesign label, has invented '*T*', a pedestal table with a folding top which can be transformed at will according to the mood of the moment. In the case of Renaud Thiry, the work's economy rests on its extrapolation of everyday commonplaces through a humorous interpretation of them. A reversal of meaning determines the reversal of the object's use and conditions the technical or formal invention involved. The *Light foot* candle which burns without dripping, the '*Up side down*' reversible vase, the lamp-cum-bookend, are all responses to this economy of reversal and displacement by subtraction. Each object's physical form balances out at the end of a process of self-

[19] The latest issue of *Les Villages* (Hazan, 1999) edited by Christine Colin is entirely devoted to the notion of comfort.

negotiation. Their combinatory mobility runs parallel to the imagining of a provisional, precarious temporality.

The '*De-Light*' table of Elsa Frances and Jean-Michel Policar represents an interface between a piece of furniture and a lamp, with no dividing line: the free-standing lampshade, without either flex or bulb, rests on the surface of the table; when turned upside down, the light goes out; if turned back the right way up, it comes on again and remains lit if it is moved around, but only on the table top.

For his part, Patrick Join has invented the '*Wonder Wall*', a standard-lamp-cum-screen which is by turns a projector screen or a light-source for image-free meditation. As a window or surface, this object combines two functions and two uses.

Morphing

Some of Join's objects or furniture pieces suggest transitional functions, such as '*Morphée*' ('Morphed/Morpheus'), a sofa-bed which represents an in-between state in the form of a morphing-style special effect. This type of imagery, as used in the films of David Cronenberg, gives a particular organic dimension to the dual-use piece. Its becoming an image (the special effect of a suggested twisting) prevails over its primary materiality. In Cronenberg's films (*Videodrome*, *eXistenZ*), the emphasis placed on object surfaces highlights zones of passage between inner and outer spaces which define forms in process of becoming. In *eXistenZ* the computer 'game pod' is alive, a type of shifting meta-flesh able to communicate with the inner body.

Morphing is literally a process of progressive digital deformation by interpolation, in order to create a different image. Special software allows each stage in the transformation of shapes and images to be observed. The idea of morphing implies a process at work which makes shapes unstable. Their surface then becomes a plane for the inscription, analysis and reading of the transformations in progress. There is a certain type of form which in itself suggests this passage from one state, one shape, to another. '*Chip*', by Teppo Asikainen and Ilkka Terho (Valvomo Design), is a chaise longue in the shape of a one-piece undulating strip which represents a provisional state, an undefined form designed to convey the idea of an in-between state of action, something between actual activity and sleep.

Patrick Jouin's creations often feature a sort of work-stage which acts as an interface between several uses or situations of space. His project for chef Alain Ducasse is an earthenware tablecloth, one corner of which is turned up to act as a knife-rest, while the centre contains a hollow to hold a plate. It looks like a wave which has been temporarily petrified.

'*Luxlab*', designed with Thierry Gaugin et Jean-Marie Massaud (1999), is at one and the same time an evolving, experimental design workshop and a manifesto for a reconsideration of the notion of luxury at the end of the 20th century. It is a rest area in the form of a self-raising grass tatami mat. The changeable floor area is made up of 4 elements. First, a stamped aluminium structure, and its covering, a (micro-capsule treated) turf layer whose shape can be distorted using jacks and pneumatic cushions. Then, hanging in the centre, an independent fireplace with Pyrex vent and vacuum filter (to allow it to be fitted in locations with no existing vent). Finally, to complete the arrangement, a 'liquid table', made of a glass top containing water which is set in motion by a pump built into the legs. A lighting system accentuates the effect of a shimmering expanse of water. This is a case where technology takes second place to a desire to create a harmonious and seductive environment which can illustrate three sensations at once: lying on the grass, looking at water, and staring into the fire. The metaphorical dimension of the statement (luxury is essentially a matter of calm and voluptuousness) is underpinned by the principle of immediate reality represented by the materials involved.

Who's Next, september 1999
entrance lock for Who's Next
Design: Matali Crasset

Ph: Matali Crasset

The 'Cosmic-thing' (1997) and sofa-bed (1998) projects also articulate interfaces and stand as responses to the 'morphing aesthetic'. Their formal register suggests provisional states and potentially multiple uses: you can stretch out, eat, read or work, all at ground level.

While Moholy-Nagy was calling drawing into question as early as 1922 in his thinking about the relationship of photography to painting, particularly with regard to his 'Telephoned Pictures' project, today's use of morphing and other computer graphics techniques updates this marginalization of drawing within design. Computerized tools intervene between the design and the finished project, acting as reflexive tools which organise a working method. The distancing of project elements caused by the use of software such as Autocad or Quark Xpress coincides with the way drawing is being called into question in contemporary design. Programming languages and creative software packages generate new conceptual procedures of dialogue between thought, hand and tool, which all interact at different speeds, but without producing automatic drawing procedures.

The generalization of computer graphics tools over the course of the 90s in the fields of design and architecture brings the issue of modelling and the identity of the creator back to the heart of thinking in those disciplines. The appearance of an 'Xpress' or 'Silicon Graphics' generation restates in a novel way the problem of the relations which come into being during the creative process between thought, representation and the object, as well as that of the modelling process which lies at the heart of all types of representation. If, in the classical theory of the Arts, the notion of model is linked to that of representation, from the start of the 20th century its meaning undergoes a shift as a result of its encounter with the regime of repetition and the economics of reproduction. It is as if the modelling process had to work on its own, for nowadays neither the sciences nor the arts are given the task of representing reality, but rather of performing operations and simulating processes. Modelling means interposing the invention of a model between reality and the act of knowing. The system of 'small wax-works' invented by Poussin offers a programmatic example: the function of these little wax models placed in perspective boxes is to produce a distancing effect for thought by presenting it with things on a different scale.

The operations of simulation and interactivity linked to the use of computers and software influence modelling towards the formulation of provisional hypotheses which help the thought-process in dialogue with itself. Computerized tools have not supplanted drawing as such, but they do introduce an extra conceptual level by generating a reflexive distance within representation itself. Drawing is thus placed in the new and wider perspective of a set of procedures which now accompany the recording of information and data processing. Apart from the fact that the intervention of these new technologies has changed the modes of conceptualization which govern the economy of works by creating new methods of modelling, information and communication technologies now play an important role in the communication of the project. The emphasis now being placed on the 'computer-assisted communication' of the project introduces a difference in degree rather than in kind from the previous working methods of designers and architects. On the other hand, the hijacking of communication mechanisms for individual promotional purposes is an operating method characteristic of certain of today's designers. The manipulation of logos as the vehicles of a brand image, the humorous manipulation of graphic signifiers which typifies digital typography, the diffusion of information across networks, correspond to a conception of the object as a communication device which turns this whole domain into a game.

Thus the RADI collective makes the misappropriation of communication codes and the ordinary uses of objects into a working method based on a general rhetoric of humour.

Humor as an Economy and Driving Force

Having decided to hide behind an acronym (Recherche-Auto-production- Design-Industriel), the members of RADI[20] have developed a very specific economy of the object in which the notion of scenarios plays a dominant role. These designers invent micro-fictions in which chatty objects dialogue above all with each other. Soliflore, designed for the 'La Vie en rose' vase exhibition at the Fondation Cartier (1998), duplicates the image of the flower by using an optical film which produces a multiple image of the vase from any angle of view. The title of their '*Fabulation*' installation designates literally the narrative and poetic programme underlying the invention of the thirty or so domestic lamps also exhibited at the Fondation Cartier (1999). Each lamp is a different height and has a shade made out of two-way mirror-glass which transforms into a light box when the lamp is switched on, showing a different picture.

The set of pieces revolve around each other to form a merry-go-round of luminous modules, making up a virtual volume and renewing accepted uses for lamps by turning them into magic lanterns which tell stories about objects and so engage the user-onlooker's imagination.

Structurally, the standard lamps in the *Fabulation* series depend on the 'double skin' principle: the pictures are drawn on a Plexiglas disk hidden inside the lamp.

In a more metaphorical sense, the double-skin principle is also seen in many other RADI creations. The extruded form of the '*Whippet*' foam-rubber sofa is shaped like a dog in profile, suggesting a humorous double-take on its shape. The blurred mirror which draws the eye right in before the reflection will focus properly also implies a process of discovery and the need for a single use. The RADI designers are in a sense creating scenarios for the gaze, setting up trompe-l'œil visual illusions which are also mind-foolers.

[20] Claude Colucci, Laurent Massaloux, Olivier Sidet, Florence Doléac-Stadler, Robert Stadler.

Their experiments are leading them to imagine typological displacements. The fireside rug called *'Sleeping cat'* (1998), put up for a Permanent Competition award from the VIA, combines the displacement of a category of objects (rug, fireplace) with a play on imagery to create an art of situation—here, dreamy restfulness.

A textile sandwich heating-element built into the rug is associated with a printed image of a cat dozing in front of the flames of an artificial fireplace. Equally, the portable phone project designed for Siemens transposes the communication vehicle (the phone) onto the body (the ankle), making a metaphorical link in terms of journeys and displacements; his imaginary telephone includes a vibrating device which is clipped into the user's shoe to warn him or her of incoming calls. The play of significations which comes about with this type of ludic, interactive object echoes the 'tamagotchi' or 'tattoo' effect: the personal communicator becomes a pet accessory which enables a very 'intimate' form of communication. The signal which it puts out interferes with the body, like some artificial prosthesis. The senses of touch, smell, hearing, and their metaphorical echoes usher in many different sensations, as in the project of a massage-mat for the soles of the feet, designed for Sommer-Allibert.

At times the identity of objects can be disturbed, as in the project for an electric switch entitled 'The Switch' (1995). The particularity of this lamp switch is that it is totally integrated into the power cable, to the point that it only works by touch: the current is turned on or off by bending the flex.

'All we did was to pick up on the symbolic aspect of a diagram of an electric switch. The switch itself is hardly visible, as it is integrated so closely into the wire. Its double-injected material makes it flexible in the middle and stiffer at the ends. The object has become no more than a sign. When the shape of the line is broken, the light goes out. The lamp, and even more the light, is the heroine of the story. Thus the object tends visually towards discretion, but it also generates a characteristic gestural pattern, and even

Il capriccio di Ugo, armchair with flap-armrests, 1998
metallic structure, cloth foam
Design: Matali Crasset
Collection "les amis de matali"
Ed: Domodinamica/Modular, Bologne
Ph: Domodinamica

sound—that of a twig snapping. So all that we have kept of the traditional switch are its pure diagrammatic logic and its sonic sensation.'

DIY and its Parody

The apparent simplicity and low-tech dimension of this object are in contrast to its technical sophistication, which ensures a perfect match between aesthetic and technical competences. This effect of a short circuit between functional efficiency and the discretion of the mechanism involved suggests a DIY economy or its parody, though one visible through objects which are designed for large-scale industrial production. This search for simplicity and anonymity brings the works of the RADI designers close to those of the Droog Design collective. However, like the Dutch designers, the RADIs are seeking to shift their and the onlooker's gaze towards the banality of everyday life by creating forms and situations which can invent a poetics of use. This coefficient of displacement of objects and functions also has a ludic aspect. RADI objects sometimes show the effects of exaggerated detail, as in the world of strange objects inhabited by Little Nemo, the character created by Windsor MacKay. The expresso cup with the stretched, outsize handle, the 'Coffee drop splash' project in which the cup is fitted with a chocolate biscuit in the crown-like shape of a splash, the candle shade which moves down as the candle burns, the armchair back which turns into a piece of a jigsaw puzzle, are all examples of imagination at work in the word of everyday objects.

Objects of Desire

The history of 20th-century art has been marked by the intrusion of objects into the artistic sphere, beginning with the 'readymades' of

Marcel Duchamp. Duchamp's move contributed to shifting the boundary between art object and manufactured object, and raised the question of the status of works of art.

The transfiguration of the banal into art and the banalization of the art object are aesthetic operations in which the exchange-value is derived from the use-value.

Situating the work of art in the broader context of mass-produced objects, or merchandise, leads to a hesitation of meaning between form and function. The resulting decontextualization gives a new autonomy to objects and works. Many of today's artists maintain an ambiguity between the object and the work of art by including furnishing elements in their works, or by suggesting that they have the function of furniture. If an object's literal meaning can be deflected or underlined by its surrounding context, any object or work can signify on two levels at once, thus setting up floating meanings. The *'Plate-formes d'objets'* ('Object Platforms') of Swetlana Heger and Planen Dejanov designate a highly porous interface between the functions of object and work of art. The design objects present on the platforms give an added symbolic value to the whole arrangement.

If modern and contemporary art have been fascinated by the object, design is in its turn fascinated by contemporary art. The symbolic super-functionality of contemporary art, particularly as in the works of Richard Artschwager, John Armleder, Jeff Koons and Haim Steinbach, creates a highly seductive effect.

The accessory-objects produced by the design industry, characterized by their multi-functionality, also have a seductive appeal as pet, attentive objects which can enter into a playful pact with their user.

Pet Objects

The projects exhibited at the 'Glassex' exhibitions in Paris and Milan by Matali Crasset, Olivier Peyricot and Xavier Moulin, dramatize a certain number of object-situations which define an evolving life-style.

Under headings such as '*Nano-architectures*', '*Hypercorners*' or '*Polymorphing*', these designers present ranges of complicit, multi-purpose objects which can move in to occupy forgotten corners in everyday spaces. '*Baladeuses*' (portable gel lamps), '*Points de rencontre*' ('Meeting Points': poufs that turns into cushion-tables), '*Saturne*' (chairs on circular rails which allow a room to be seen from different points of view), are all inventing experimental protocols, driven by humour, for thinking up new ways of filling leisure time and occupying private space. The proposals of Matali Crasset, Olivier Peyricot et Xavier Moulin display a discreet type of 'stealth design' which places the user at the centre of a platform of information and uses, blurring the dividing line between public and private space, free time and work time. The '*Smartphone*' is a Nokia prototype which allows the user to surf the Web, make phone calls, order a meal in a restaurant of his or her choice, or send and receive email messages and pictures. The Gemplus microchip '*Easywatch*', worn on the wrist, transmits information stored on the chip to receivers which pick up electronic money transactions or visiting card details. GPS receivers, smart mice, headphones and '*Webpad*'-type personal communicators are preparing the individual of tomorrow to become a fully-interactive subject.

RADI objects tell us about their own propensity to become objects of desire by setting up numerous playful pacts with the user in order to create new modes of user-friendliness. The way the creations of the RADI group tend towards the accessory makes them into 'pet objects,' to use the designers' own term. The function of pet objects is to accompany everyday living yet displace people's perception of it to the point of becoming 'parasitic' on it and stealing its codes.

The theme of parasitism is a recurrent one in the wok of the RADI group. It operates on three levels: in a literal and material sense, it can be seen at work in their prototype for an attaché case in polystyrene and topstitched leather, in which the handle in the shape of a short sleeve covers the hand up to the wrist, suggesting a partial artificial limb. On a metaphorical or poetic level, parasitic objets are multi-functional ones: the crown-shaped chocolate biscuit in the '*Coffee drop splash*' project is parasitic on the coffee cup, in that it adds an additional motif which amplifies the object's basic function. Finally, the parasite notion also operates in relation to a play on references to contemporary art. Numerous allusions to Robert Gober, Wim Delvoye, Magritte, Marin Kasimir, Philippe Ramette, Bertrand Lavier, Markus Retz, Fischli et Weiss... form a short history of modern art. An ironic use of misapplied and indirect quotations defines a practice of 'second-hand' works whose aim is to invent a singular economy for the design of objects and products, the main elements of which are displacement, changes of perspective, and the conceptual dimension of proposals, as well as language games. In the work of the RADI group, the way objects are made to become fictions determines a working method by establishing a singular methodology of production, publishing and distribution.

Micro-scenarios from everyday life and its patterns of usage structure both the content of objects, and their mode of production, which thus takes on an experimental dimension.

New Technologies: Real Science-Fiction

New technologies applied to the field of materials, images and communication have introduced new procedures of creation and production into industry, the media and design. Ways of thinking that are contemporaneous with modelling, virtuality, and automated design and production procedures, lead one to imagine novel types of experiments which are a cross between pure technological research, industry and design.

Because of the invention of new synthetic materials made possible by polymer technology, matter has taken on a new dimension. In his essay *'La matière de l'invention'* ('The Matter of Invention') (1989), Ezio Manzini points out that the invention of new shape-memory materials is leading to the creation of models expressive of a system where identities are becoming blurred and change is gaining the upper hand over stability. This new paradigm ushers in new types of rationality: variability and the fluctuations in current processes signal a crisis of the subject and of western reason. The designing of objects with highly integrated functions testifies to the non-uniqueness of forms of reasoning and the non-linearity of design processes. Project design is now affected by the question of technological limitations and competences. With synthetics the relationship between empirical observation, knowledge of materials and the study of their performance becomes indirect.

In this context, Manzini has for a number of years been working on a project for a prototype submarine which involves a proposed technological displacement of the relationship between water and vacuum. The function of this creative metaphorical transfer is to provide a foundation for new representational models and to respond to hitherto unseen possibilities created by new technological skills.

In the work of Jean-Marie Massaud, the interaction of design with new technologies leads to the emergence of a creative universe tinged with science-fiction. Like the screenplays of *'Star Trek'* which literally dramatize imaginary scientific and technological developments in a future society, Jean-Marie Massaud's researches are leading him to experiment with every possible way in which design could appropriate the new synthetic shape-memory materials. In his *'O'Azar'* (a pun on 'By Chance') chair (1996), he has imagined a paradoxical meeting between wood (in the form of slats) and nitrogen-injected polypropylene. The association between these two interlocking technologies of different levels of complexity gives a minimalist object which is extremely light. Though he avoids the question of use, which he does not contest, Jean-Marie Massaud still succeeds in renewing the image of this object of furniture. The idea highlighted here is the encounter between cut out wood and moulded plastic, the juxtaposition of fragment with overall shape.

The decontextualization procedure that underlies the design economy of these pieces implies in particular that the object as such is not an end in itself: it belongs to a larger system in which it is only one element, on the model of the situation and status of objects in science-fiction stories.

In an unpublished text, Jean-Marie Massaud describes both his conception of design and the identity of objects today: '*Progress tends to replace matter with energy: electrons have replaced the pendulum, waves the mail-coach, pre-stressed cellular construction solid materials. When an object's intelligence is concentrated in an increasingly virtual mechanism, we need to learn how to construct that void and give it a meaning of its own. We might then hypothesize a legitimate object stripped to its essentials in terms of materials, use and meaning.*'

His current project for *O'Azar*, a unisex jacket, is a response to this progressive clarification of the elements that go into the creative process. The jacket is '*basic, timeless, able to be worn in the day as well as the evening. In fact, as with my other projects, I have cleaned up the product and stripped it down to its simplest expression.*'

For his exhibition at the Musée des arts Décoratifs in January 1999, he created a set of furnishing-objects which dramatize an imaginary techno scenario. '*Horizontal memory*' is a modular shelving system in expanded polyethylene foam and luminous colors which alludes equally to the structure of memory and to rhizome-shaped printed circuits. '*Dark light*' is a light made of plastic net.

'*Horizontal chair*' is a chaise longue made out of techno-polymer sheeting covered with a protein-based self-healing skin developed with the help of TS TECH Japan and produced by E & Y, also in Japan. Jean-

Work at home, domestic office furniture, 1996
Design: Matali Crasset
Carte blanche V.I.A

Ph: Dominique Feintrenie

Marie Massaud's way of working is to 'remain subservient to the object's usage', so as to 'construct the void.'

'*Horizontal chair*' is an attempt to achieve a highly radical effect by calling on the most sophisticated of technology: '*I use a material developed by Yamaha for car seats: a self-healing foam rubber that adapts to body temperature. I have played on the contrast between the lightness of the seat, like a levitating leaf, and the heavy stainless-steel ingot across which it is fixed.*' The working drawing of the seat line as is translated by the materials used underlines the function of a chaise longue: the horizontal line alludes to the siesta, a brief spell of light daytime sleep, or other moments of rest or idleness.

Matali Crasset also makes clear how she sees the interface between design and the new technologies as applied to industry and creation:

"*In some projects for instance, like those for which I use FIT, a thermoplastic impregnated fibre, in combination with a metallic structure that will give the material rigidity, I am moving into creative practices which are a mixture of craftsmanship and technology. I think this is something that will be carefully studied in years to come, because people are realizing that industrialists can no longer afford to put in huge investments, but are forced to find what I call short cuts.*'[21]

In this text, Matali Crasset points out one of the designer's functions with respect to the development of new technologies in the field of design. While it is no doubt true that the new image and communication technologies have succeeded in recent years in familiarizing the general public with contemporary art, designers perhaps now have the task of shadowing the integration of new technologies into industry, helping creative people to make appropriate use of them, and fostering their wide-spread dissemination into the social sphere by drawing up specifications and doing concept designs.

[21] *Design 10 ans*, Saint-Etienne, Ecole des Beaux-Arts Editeur, septembre 1998, p. 104.

Little Inventory for a Networked Reality. The World's Time

The development of the Internet and the globalization of exchanges over the last decade have made the culture of virtuality into a reality and created the necessity to develop a political economy of new technologies in respect of the construction of a new type of public space. The extension of this amorphous grouping onto a global level, and the explosion of the Web, raise a number of issues. For instance, we do not yet know enough about how private use of the Internet affects the mechanisms of subjectivization and individuation by which subjects appropriate an imaginary social and ideological sphere, to see whether there are specific phenomena involved. We might ask what types of representation could be imagined on the Web, if indeed that is what is happening. We might wonder on what basis to imagine the constitution of our image of the world, and how far we can experiment with that representation, while in the absence of any fixed mechanism, the Web operates rather like a magic slate: on the Web, everything rises to the surface, but it can also be wiped clean. The key question is what displacements can be brought about by creative works, and how to inscribe memory durably onto the surface of a magic slate.

The world's time is increasingly affected nowadays by the speed of tele-technologies which are eating into private time. Cosmopolitan Chinese artist Chen Zen perfectly captures the de-synchronization of time and space which is overtaking the body of the world and the body of history:

'*We are living through a time of multiple dislocations: between natural nature and the nature that man is constantly producing and inventing; between the generations; between those who know about computers and make daily use of them and those who have no access; between the speed of consumption and the existential limitations of nature; between the body and mind of man as a unit, a unit at least under constant challenge from the omnipresence of speed. Ultimately, man has only made gains in the speed of his technologies, not in the depth of his thinking or his intelligence. We gain through faster production times, rather than by using the extra time to think through the project and its design more thoroughly. People are wrong when they assume that thinking can be speeded up. What we lack is a sort of void in the Taoist sense of the term, to help us concentrate better and think more deeply.'*[22]

The eulogy of slowness that is conveyed by Chen Zen's text is not incompatible with the art of interactive narrative generated by certain video games.

In his latest film, *eXistenZ*, which looks at this theme, David Cronenberg adopts from the start the position of an onlooker: *'I don't take sides, I reason like a scientist conducting an experiment. I look at what happens. I believe in the film's philosophy, which is that we must all create out own reality. For me, all reality is virtual, so we can choose our own.'*

As in all his previous films, Cronenberg examines here the relationship between reality and technology, with emphasis on the presence of the real world and of the body as flesh. He analyses the nature of video games and their status as representation and inter-personal communication interfaces, adopting an original perspective which does not deny the involvement of the body in the technical set-up.

The notion of video games implies an arrangement involving screens and a computerised environment based on programmed rules and simulation. Live interaction takes place between the player's actions and behaviour and the computer's validation or otherwise of his or her progress through the game.

Like robots in the field of artificial intelligence and robotics, video games can be used to simulate operations in the real world. One initially

[22] Chen Zen, in *'Gare de l'Est'* catalogue, Casino du Luxembourg, 1999, p. 34-35.

unforeseen use of such games would be to critique and manage the virtual realities which have been invading our everyday living-space over the last decade. The existence of a virtual flip-side to reality may paradoxically bring us closer to the real world by allowing us to question it more thoroughly.

If reality is in essence virtual, that virtuality works at the level of procedures and contexts, without affecting the reality of objects. Following the injunctions to 'rematerialize' or 'dematerialize' which dominated the 1970s and 80s, the task as we leave the 20th century behind may now be to found a new operative realism, on the basis of the critical hypotheses that can be formulated about the world as it is.

The role of design objects is perhaps now to construct hypotheses, take sides and set out political options, since the relationship between thought and technology is, from start to finish, an ideological matter. To become in a fundamental way our tools for analyzing reality. To be the black boxes of the world.

Oritapi, 2D/3D carpet (prototype), 1999
cut out felt
Design: Matali Crasset
Glassex project

Ph: Lon Van Keulen

Nouvelle Vague

*I*nquiring persons to end up not mentioning them seems a bit illogical, but it's exactly what we wanted here. It's not the personality though strong and passionate, of each of these designers we are trying to describe. The international press takes care of that every day. It's not their work we want to show either, the numerous exhibitions to which they participate will do so in a more exhaustive manner. But through their answers we find a portrait of a singular generation that, today, holds the capital interest of the ensemble of a profession that asks itself why and how they got there.

Actually France is not the country of design. French contemporary work is almost inexistant, the specialised press a bit too nostalgic; the design market is more or less equivalent to that of a third world country. The word itself, design, doesn't seem to design much in people's mind here. So, is it an accidental reality from a spontaneous generation, or should we see major changes in engagements, attitudes, and manner.

Now, let's talk about Starck. Since the title of this piece might suggest that he should be, once again, the one concerned.

One common point that shared Matali Crasset, Patrick Jouin, Jean-Marie Massaud, Frédérique Valette, Mathilde Brétillot, Beef, is that they all had collaborated with Philippe Starck. A few days for some, several years for others, no matter. Which is obviously the reason why chose them.

Philippe Starck marked in France, and the world, a rupture in the recent history of design. More than his work, it was his behaviour that changed this history. So much that, as in every revolution, we can safely say that there exists a pre-Starck, and a post-Starck. Like Johnny Rotten or Andy Warhol, his actions were not just that of an evolution of a practice, an art form, or a profession, but it transformed this practice into a genuine culture.

Using the system to dismantle it, taking maximum advantage of the media, laying the foundations of a global culture by building bridges between art, fashion, music and cinema, design eventually passed from the state of the lab coat industrial aesthetics, to the flamboyant new design state. With its own stars, myths on success, and dreams of 'anything is possible'.

This transformation was in the nature of things. It would have occured anyway, the way it happened in all cutural disciplines. Except that Starck has genuinely crystalized it, materialised it and certainly accelerated it.

Post-Starck then, here we are. A few talented young designers, talented enough for Starck to notice and hire, regain their independence and put together a personal work of art based on the ideas and values they will share.

It' s this shared domain, these new ideas they federate, that we wanted them to express. It's also, between the lines, to distinguish how this generation uses its heritage.

I interviewed, very freely, each of these persons present in this opening. Sometimes, certain questions orientated the answers towards a specific idea, an idea clearly present in each of their work. More often starting off very vague, the subjects appeared by themselves in a recurrent manner, according to the different conversations. I merely put together in a nomenclature these answers or bits of these conversations.

Show Business

Matali Crasset

The media are "designer-eaters". They need to put the light on somebody. I happen to be a woman and, since originating from the countryside, a satellite in the business. I think this is more than sufficient to create a sort of curiosity, that makes people look at me and question me.

What is also interesting is the fact that people are more inclined to identify a process than projects. This is a new way of judging people. Creating a huge quantity of products is not required anymore to arouse curiosity or interest. If the process remains constant, if a will for working in different fields can be perceived, I think this can be a new way of observing and evaluating. A sort of transversality. I think this has had a great deal to do with it. My work for Thomson also seems intriguing. My professional past with Starck. A whole range of things that, being added to each other, create a singular profile.

First, my communiqué shouldn't be considered as advertising, but as the expression of a desire (that we all have) to transmit things and ideas that seem either important or essential to us. This is the reason why we produce exhibitions, that we present projects that might never be edited, but that contain in an explicit way, what motivates us, what commits us.

Mathilde Brétillot, Frédérique Valette

Today we live in a system in which a designer is supposed to be a good speaker, a good writer, and has to be photogenic, has to be pleasant. What he is, is as important as what he does. A designer is a 'trade mark'. Take Matali Crasset for example, unfortunately people hardly know her products, but her logo is everywhere. This is very representative of what design is today, intrinsically linked to a person. There is no place anymore for the obscure industrial designer who creates his objects in a studio. Today, the designer has to be a star to have orders made. It is a very show-biz like system.

Jean Marie Massaud

To pretend that my last exhibition at the museum of Decorative Arts has something of a retrospective is first untrue and then embarrassing for me.

The story of this exhibition is really a very simple story. I organised it to please Yoichi Nakamuta, who wanted to show, in Paris, the long-chair I had drawn for him.

I first got in touch with galerists, something I am certainly not good at, but as soon as I told them it was all about a Japanese publisher, they immediately alluded to the price of 2 million dollars. I eventually tried the institutions, and when the 'Arts Déco' finally gave me the green light, I wasn't allowed to fail. I knew I had to do a little bit more than to simply show three long-chairs.

It has absolutely nothing to do with narcissism. I have not wanted my work to be seen in an emblematic way, but as soon as the exhibition takes place in such a museum, you have to prove your merit.

I have not yet produced a lot of things. This was the occasion to create new models, to show some new ideas. It is true it was also the occasion to show myself. But I absolutely don't have the PR feeling, that suits this show-biz side of my profession. I am quite shy. And if you want to work with interesting companies, you have to show not only what you do, but also show what you are.

Today, it is the media that open the door to the publishing companies by editing your work. Even if you have no media strategy, which is my case, once your face has been seen several times in the press, people come up with a different attitude towards you. It is generally assumed that it is the value of the project that makes his author famous and arouses curiosity, in fact, it is rather the contrary. Even if I think it is a pity, even if I have no desire to be included in that system, I cannot deny that an exhibition is part of it.

I think eulogising a designer is a pretty insane thing. Anyway, I prefer spending my time drawing projects.

Beef

We are rather discrete persons. I can't see anything in our behaviour that could be assimilated to any kind of self promotion. The world of graphic design is different from the world of design.

There is no graphic-design star, apart from maybe Neville Brody in the eighties.

Much more than design, graphic-design is linked to fashion, to trends. And like trends, if you have too much of a desire to show and show off, to impose an image, a style, you are consumed and become old fashioned very easily. Graphic design is here to serve an image, not to substitute for it.

Origins

Jean Marie Massaud

As a kid, for a long time, I used to read all sorts of 'Géo Trouvetout' manuals, books on inventions or experiments of all kind. I wanted to be an inventor.

Then I practised sports, more precisely, I studied sport. It was a way of easing my conscience. I wasn't doing much, while pretending I was studying.

Then I registered at the university to become an aeronautical engineer. Creating planes, that was like chasing after the passions of my childhood.

But I soon realised I would finally end up at 50 years old, wearing a grey lab coat, making calculations on the circulation of fluids in hydraulic systems.

Far from the work of an inventor.

I entered by chance at the Workshops in Paris, only because I had seen a picture showing a man in bermuda shorts, in the sun, surrounded by inventive machines and computers. I said to myself, that's it, it's right that.

What must me remembered of it, is this blend of laziness and fascination for sciences.

Matali Crasset

My parents are farmers. I was born in a village of 80 inhabitants.

For many reasons, the time I spent at Thomson's is a determining experience. It first enabled me to have a privileged relationship with Starck who, outside the context of his office, was very open to discussions on important and deep ideas concerning the work we were carrying on.

And then, I was immersed in a technological universe that is the one that truly fascinates me.

Finally, this experience has been a sort of life experience. Our projects focussed on the general public. We worked for the people, with the people, for a mass production. This particular dimension is generally not accesible to young designers. I think this stay at Thomson's was a strong concentrate of different things that today have an influence on my relationships with customers.

Beef

(Sébastien): I entered the Beaux-Arts (Fine Arts School) to take my revenge on school. As much as I was bad at school, I had the will to excell in creation. It is not a judgment on work but on my state of mind. I entered the Beaux-Arts at fifteen. A lot of derogations have been necessary to do so. Then I left to England. Beef was born within the Thomson team where I met Simon.

(Simon): I have always drawn and I have always wanted to do nothing but to draw. I considered school as a temporary obligation. I've never done more than the strict minimum, waiting for the time I would be old enough to enter the Beaux-Arts.

Mathilde Brétillot, Frédérique Valette

(Mathilde): I come from a family in which the relationships that link us are almost tribal. They are so strong, so reassuring that it modifies my relationship with the outside world. This feeling is not easily understood, but I believe it influences the value I attach to my relationship with the others. It is of a great importance. It thus has an influence on the way I practise my profession.

(Frédérique): I think I don't have anything particular to mention about this. No… Nothing. Very normal. Petit-bourgeois small-town girl.

Eclectism

Jean Marie Massaud

I easily get bored if I have to do the same thing several times. If I'm a designer, it's because I have the feeling that I'm doing a different job every day.

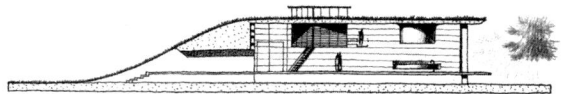

Tanabe House (sections), 1998
ongoing project
Fukuoka, Japon
Design: Jean-Marie Massaud

Besides, I can't stand people with great dogmas. It seems to me quite fruitless. It eradicates a whole part of reality. As for me, I stand in contexts that vary according to the projects I'm tackling. The solutions I find also vary. For example, I wouldn't deal with the project of a house the same way I would deal with the project of a building. According to me, these worlds are not of the same kind. They define very different contexts. I have no quest nor great cause I could fight for in the way I practise my work, but I do have micro points of view on things, and it is in accordance with them that I tackle each object I consider.

I think changing all the time is in y nature.

I am not a chameleon, but rather one day a fish and the other a bird. Very human desires, after all.

Patrick Jouin

I think having no unmistakable style is something one should wish for. I find amusing that people are unable to identify a designer thanks to his style, that they can't immediately understand what it is all about. It is the object, what truly matters, that is more looked at than the person who designed it. And right now, having a style is not something I care about. It remains to be seen later, when lots of things will have been done. Maybe then something will come out. Today I don't look at what has been done previously, I'm not looking for a continuity, it is a bit as if I was at each time a different designer.

It doesn't mean doing one thing and the contrary. But today, all disciplines are mixed up. A designer plays different parts: artist, movie director, stage designer. Take you for example, you are designer, and yet, you are now playing the part of a journalist. What you do, what you think about, doesn't take a unique form, in a unique practice. It is a very sensitive thing, always the same, but that expresses itself in all fields possible. It is far from the expression of a style. It is more the definition of a spirit or a nature.

Mathilde Brétillot, Frédérique Valette

Nowadays, designers are thought of as being more eclectic than before. But who knows whether persons such as Sottsas or others have had versatile periods or not. They might have been very eclectic before imposing an image that represents them today. Who knows. Imposing a drawing or an image is not an easy thing to do. But is it better to draw a kettle that would look like a table? Is it better to always draw the same line in order to be recognised? Isn't it an artifice stuck on an object? I think it might be more interesting to be recognised not for a style but for a way of working, a way of thinking. I believe it is also interesting to keep with a certain ingenuity at each time a new context is dealt with or discovered. Just as if we were always to wipe the slate clean.

Anyway, your own style always comes out intuitively. There is no need to make it come through. It may seem airy, or fickle, but we do live in a fickle society. Why should we always put the same things in the same boxes. As for us, we work in a happy-go-lucky fashion.

We don't have a linear practise because we don't look for any kind of relationship between our projects. What makes the unity is the person who 'designs', not an artifice displayed afterwards.

Matali Crasset

The idea of a personality built up around a single centre of interest or one form of expression is not current anymore. A designer can be 'multiple', and this is inevitably reflected in his projects. So it's true it has all become much more complicated. Before, there were boxes in which we were neatly arranged. Today, we all fit in all the boxes. It is not the symptom of a lack of motivation but rather the expression of multidirectional motivation. We can also bring different messages at each time we deal with different projects. Simply because the context is different, because the destination is different. In the past, people were specialised in one subject, today we want to be present in a whole range of sectors.

Beef

Even if it has evolved now, the frontiers between the disciplines are still very 'hermetic'. The 'professional fields' still don't blend very well. I can't see much eclectism. There is a certain unity in our work. Our referential basis is certainly very wide, but we never work in forms of expression that would be 'distant' from one another. The eclecticism would most likely be found in the nature of our projects, of our orders.

Culture

Jean-Marie Massaud

I think it is necessary to be aware of what has been previously done, in order not to state the obvious. Unfortunately I am not a cultivated person. When I entered the School of the Ateliers, and when I was asked in an interview who my favourite designers were, I felt a huge emptiness. I didn't know any of them. Not even Starck.

I'm a very curious person, and I'm always intrigued by certain domains, like architecture for example, I realise everyday how much this curiosity doesn't engender any form of knowledge to my account.

I always keep myself out of the publishing, the media, the books, even if I like spending time appreciating the determining ideas some, the ones I call the masters, have brought up.

Enzo Mari, for better or for worse. The better, that's the striking presence of the material, the elegance in its simplest expression, beyond the style, thanks to an extremely simple vocabulary. The work is also inevitably fraught with emotion.

Rizatto is very often associated with Meda because he also has the attitude of staying in the background. As a result, it is the product that takes precedence over all the rest. This is of an exemplary honesty, so far from the show-biz attitude. Charles Eames also. An absolute must.

Mathilde Brétillot

We use our awareness to create bridges between different practices. Our knowledge stands more on a sensitive level than on an analytical one.

We fill our design projects with analogical impressions referring to certain literary texts. But once again, it is not a very analytical culture, it rather belongs to a field of impressions.

More than culture, it is curiosity that matters. What interests us is the idea of discovering, much more than the idea of acquiring knowledge. We don't look in one precise direction, or with a precise idea in mind.

It is also important, beyond the tastes that one can have for a cultural practice, to understand the reason why a person works in a given direction.

Finding references, or a reflection in terms of positioning or commitment is what matters.

We find our inspiration in many artists. Rather English, like Deacon, Cragg, Amish Kappour... People whose masterpieces are at the same time extremely clear and very complex when related to the context.

In the literary field, it is an author I regularly read, that inspires me: Christian Bobin. There is no plot in his novels, but each sentence opens on a painting.

As well as many unknown persons we love for the fragment of one thing, for a detail...

Patrick Jouin

My culture is a mixture of techniques and mechanics that gather around the idea of 'brainwave'. I think I've been brought up (my father is a craftsman/engineer) with the idea that the creation of an object is justified by the intervention of intelligence, by a 'brainwave'.

My culture, that's also contemporary art: Alan Vexler, Dennis Hoppenheim, Gonzales Forester. I'm more inclined to installation.

I think music is the most powerful means of expression. I like experimental music: Steve Reich, and remixes of Steve Reich's music, if there are some. It's only in music that I appreciate the minimalism I'm associated with.

Minimalism is often perceived as a form of way out to avoid the notion of style. I do think minimalism is in fact the most acute form of style: objects that want to disappear but that are in fact noisy with their sole presence.

Matali Crasset

I don't consider myself to be very cultivated. As far as culture is concerned, I've started out with a slight handicap. Back home, reading is a waste of time. In the agricultural world, there are so many things to do, that reading meant not doing what should be done.

I've acquired culture late in life, a very selective culture, fatally made of small parcels.

Today, references and quotations are more 'homeopathic'. They are used in mixtures or mixings of micro-scraps. There is no trace today of this sort of unique reference, this unique source of inspiration that would direct a whole work of art.

My main source is art. Artists have more freedom in terms of expression and are thus more up to creating a whole material of reflection.

I really enjoy the exhibitions on young painters where the work of artists that might still be at school is presented. Most of the time, it is patched up and knocked up. But there is food for thought. Otherwise, concerning well-established artists, it is not the work as a whole that will attract my attention but sometimes insignificant details, parts.

There is also a whole unidentifiable range of things in cinema and music, that constitute an important source of inspiration for me, but the exact influence of which I'm unable to figure out. Fashion doesn't make much sense to me. I think it requires a decoder I don't have yet, unless it is my decoder that is not on the right wavelength.

The more you intervene in the cultural field, the more you have the chance of being misunderstood. For instance, I had drawn with Starck a radio that was in fact a head in the Brancusi style. At Thomson's, everybody used to call it the mouse! Nobody had seen the rather explicit reference. Culture can be exclusive, partly because, we don't have the same culture.

It is necessary to find other forms of access for people, other channels to reach everybody. I think the dimension of feelings should not be ignored. What people will feel. The field of my investigations rather stands there, in the empathy, and less in the transmission of cultural codes. In my case, it is expressed through the small things of everyday life. Things we've all lived with, things from our childhood, childish impressions, that I rework and I inject in the product to provide this feeling, an emotion that can be shared by everybody.

Motivation

Jean Marie Massaud

I am not a theorist, and I repeat, I have no quest. My taste is not very discerning and I'm influenced by a lot of things that can seem contradictory. I have no opinion to impose, but intuitions that I would rigorously formulate.

Horizontal Memory (net), shelves, 1999
expanded polyethylen, prototype
Design: Jean-Marie Massaud
Ed: Magis, Italie

Ph: Jean-Marie Massaud Studio

Untitled, flap-miror (project)
silvered curved glass
Design: Jean-Marie Massaud

Ph: Jean-Marie Massaud Studio

Dark light, standard lamps, 1998
bulpren foam filter and lacquered metal
Design: Jean-Marie Massaud

Ph: Mario Pignata Monti

Design is made to make children's dreams come true, to materialise desires and fantasies, that enable us to escape from daunting everyday life. It is meant to build a world of emotion, of pleasure and freedom.

Building an underwater house, for example, or a tree house…

It is made to free us from gravity.

Mathilde Brétillot, Frédérique Valette

Design today is meant to make people happy. It is funny to be involved in the life of people we will never get to know.

Patrick Jouin

Design should be the expression of intelligence. What we know best. It is very human. It simply is the idea of going beyond search. We don't need all that, but we can't do anything but trying to go beyond it. We look for the Unbelievable matter that urges us to search, forever. Take the clockworks for example, it is phenomenal. It goes far beyond the functional research.

As far as I'm concerned, this justification is sufficient.

Matali Crasset

What may seem something like self-promotion to some, is in fact a deep and important thing to me: sharing.

At each time I'm working on a project, I let people see it because it seems important to me to exchange; to share what it is made of. I think there is a real problem. There are not enough transmissions, it is a wrong way of functioning. And it is a bad image of it.

Showing my work is not a planned strategy, it is natural. When I deal with a project, I have to show what I'm working on. A project is not finished if it has not been seen by anyone.

I've always tried to have personal experiences, with the furniture for example. I think it is important to develop, to invent new typologies in the furniture field. There is a something established and fossilised in the creation of furniture that is contrary to the necessity to evolve. It is only the surface of things that is changed, but the structure itself has never been questioned, despite the evolution of our life style.

There is a huge gap between our desire to live in a different manner and the way people really live at home.

Beef

We are motivated by a will to reach the greatest number of persons possible, to collaborate in the widest areas possible, but the motivation is not a quest for success. Above all, it is a desire to share our ideas, our desires, our own world. There is also the pleasure to 'infiltrate' sectors, or companies that are in the first place, very far from our means of expression.

We have more in common in process and attitude with the music world than with the business world. This is truly how our desire to share and gather should be understood.

Innovation

Jean-Marie Massaud

Innovation has for me a lot to do with modernity. That is to say never being satisfied with the achievements, and systematically questioning what surrounds us. I believe innovation is today more on the level of what we bring in behaviours, in people's way of life, more than on the level of the performance and the quality standards of the object.

Concerning furniture for example, the creative process has remained stuck in its own typologies. Even if its means of production has never ceased evolving, benefiting from the latest discoveries and technological inventions, a chair is still today a chair, like in the time of interior decorators. Innovation lies in this questioning.

Innovation is not used anymore for the sake of 'a better life', but rather of 'a different life'. The innovations I can try and work on in my practice have a prior finality: my idea of well-being, my idea of pleasure in life, one form of hedonism.

SESA 570, submarin project (5m70*2m44), 1990/93 (ongoing project)
fuselage (stratified époxy; glass and kevlar) windows (polymetacrylat) structure
(stainless steel pipes) axial motor, lead batteries
autonomy: usual mission 8 hours, secured 120 hours
3 potential passengers
varied equipments: surface radio, GPS position system, tunx satellite, panoramic
sonar, 600w projector
Design: Jean-Marie Massaud

Ph: Olivier Cadouin

Mathilde Brétillot, Frédérique Valette

Drawing a form in relation with aesthetical or technical criteria is not what matters today. Innovation doesn't lie in the object anymore, but in the context it either represents or projects. What is innovating is your position, not the object that thus becomes more of a medium. Today we are not given articles and conditions. But you have to understand to whom you are talking, what this person needs and desires. Innovation is contained in the relationship, and less in the object itself.

Being cynical, one could say that true innovation today lies in the fact that objects need more to be told about than made or loved. An important object is an object that is published in the magazines. The others simply don't exist. We'd rather keep on making nice drawings and nice products.

Patrick Jouin

Innovation can't be found in the drawing of an object but in the use that is made of technology, materials, techniques. Technology has no interest for its image, but it is interesting for the service it offers. Its image must disappear, melt into the object. Technology is at the service of the result: price, lightness, comfort...

I've designed a walkman jacket for Thomson. It is the demonstration of my opinion. Electronics completely disappear. The service ' listen to the music' only remains. The image of the machine has disappeared.

The more technology, the less technological objects. Only the indispensable objects remain: the ones that are related to the primary human functions: sleeping, eating...

The bed I've drawn for Roset, that's exactly what I'm heading to. Everybody understands that it suggests another way of living in a house. It implies freedom in the use people will make of it. It is not a TV set, a sofa, or a table, but something vague, less definite.

Innovation also lies in typology. 'Typology', that's a trendy word. New typology, that sounds a bit seventies-like. It's because we find the same generosity again today, the same desire for utopias. Company owners were young, and they enjoyed building and innovating. Objects were not vain, they would come to the people. The number of uncomfortable chairs created in the eighties is symbolical of the eighties, as well as the will of not making uncomfortable chairs in the nineties is symbolical of the nineties. Typology is more linked to the renewal of shapes than to the idea of the improvement of either ergonomics or comfort. The idea that typology would fit in with something scientific is an old-fashioned idea. It requires precaution.

Matali Crasset

I try to make objects that would represent a way of thinking or a proposition regarding a life style. The object has less importance for itself and more importance in its symbolical dimension or in its function as a transmitter of ideas. It is considered as a transmitter, or rather the materialisation of a way of thinking.

The hierarchy in the values of a piece of furniture has changed. The importance of its own qualities such as comfort, style, and aesthetics doesn't prevail any longer. The major quality is today more contained in the expression of a new life style, in the proposition of an alternative concerning our behaviours.

I think this is all about a new order of values and their evolution full of nuances rather than the apparition of new values. The objects keep their traditional values but there are different proportionings. There is always an amount of money put up front. There are always stakes on status, but it takes different shades. Today, it is less about 'how much I earn' and more about 'how intelligent I am'.

Beef

Breaking the rules is the driving force of innovation in our profession. The innovation is not contained in an image, in a font, in a composition, but rather in the way these elements question all conformisms and certainties. The innovation doesn't lie in the form, it lies in the gap created by this form on an object that is not supposed to take it on. In the feeling of openness and freedom that is produced by this alternative.

Morals

Patrick Jouin

Morals in design has something dishonest. Anyway I find discussing honesty a very dishonest thing. Not that I think the ideas that are fought for are uninteresting, but people often proclaim as grand ideas, things that are just after all, the qualities expected about an object. What an object owes us.

Ecology, for example, is not a 'grand idea', but a need that is induced by any industrial project. The democratisation of design, that is to say creating cheaper objects, that is not a deed of good will. Making things more accessible, that means selling more. It means more money to be earned.

The aim of design is to express and tell a story, a poem. Morals. That's where honesty is, in the existence and importance of this content.

Mathilde Brétillot, Frédérique Valette

'Morals', that's a word that has recently reappeared in design. The whole idea is, I think, that the objects become human; they have a soul and therefore, morality. Our feeling is that such an idea smells like marketing. It is the contrary of morals. It is a lack of respect. It is non-respect.

The work that is a demonstration of so-called moral ideas, that's very dull. Obsolete. There can't be just one moral, it inevitably comes up against another one, a different one. It's like pretending there would be only one way of thinking.

If morals were to keep us from making objects, we would never design an object or a project for morals sake.

Jean-Marie Massaud

Morals, that's just a few guiding rules that you impose on yourself to live in harmony with your environment: sincerity, politeness, respect, honesty… Going on a crusade for it is derisory. Advocating the honest object, the moral object, the respectful object, the sociable object, advocating the politically-correct object that fits established standards, I find it suspicious. I like the acceptation of differences, I love this kind of freedom. Then an object is not dangerous, people always have the choice not to buy it.

Human

Patrick Jouin

The idea of progress is dead today. The idea of technical and scientific progress, the modern idea of Bauhaus, according to which the human being would reach happiness thanks to the progress of techniques is not sufficient anymore. Today, there is a human, chaotic, disorganised, 'messy' part that would be the essence of happiness.

There is in the objects from the eighties a totemic and caricatured part, but so sincere with the human quality that is expressed. This deep human part is very touching. After all I find this very honest because it concerns what should be done. It has been overdone, but it is decent.

Jean-Marie Massaud

I believe the human factor is the 'raison d'être' of my profession. I don't work to make machines, or to make machines build machines. I draw for myself, for us, in order to live a better life. It is not a grand idea, but only our reason to do so.

The human feeling today, is not the quest for the ultimate product, it is not the heroic idea of going beyond our condition. It is contained in things that remain inside of ourselves: imperfection, humour, laziness, fragility, versatility... What is human, is considering the person in its singularity, in its intimacy. The human being is neither a stereotyped unity in a global system, nor an abstract idea, but a real physical and existing being.

Mathilde Brétillot, Frédérique Valette

Speaking about what is human, willing to be at the service of what is human: by saying such things, one makes himself stand out from the crowd, being the anthropologist of the others. There is something that slightly bothers us in this consideration, something in the order of disdain. We don't target a genre, but persons, one single person. We don't have the impression that we aim at the mass. The human dimension lies in the exchange, in a sensual and lyrical attention that we can transmit thanks to our practice. The human factor, that is maybe also what comes clear when one is trying to be as sincere as possible, as implied as possible as far as the others are concerned. But above all, we don't pretend to target everybody. We don't create products for everybody, but we do think on the contrary, that we may please some people.

Design

Beef

Design, we don't really know what that means. It is a word that has become a sort of label in the public domain. I remember the presentation of a project designed for a big cosmetics brand. The person in charge acclaimed her joy, 'it's very Porsche design', she said. Although we laughed heartedly, we were very embarrassed. Design, that also reminds me of this magazine in the eighties: Newlook. It was a slightly vulgar magazine. I don't know why I associate it with anything 'very design'.

Patrick Jouin

Design. That is the worst insult that could qualify a product: 'that's so design'. It means it's ruined!

Design is something that should not be noticed. A well drawn product is a fluid product, in which the intention is not felt. A product that imposes itself without signature, without noise. Like the Meda and Rizzato lamp, perfect, much more important than the Archimoon lamp by Starck. I think it's important not to try and obtain any artificial style.

Mathilde Brétillot, Frédérique Valette

Design doesn't mean anything to us, it doesn't mean anything anymore. In the past, Louis XIV-style, Louis XV-style, Louis-XVI-style, that was design. These objects were representative of something that respected the rules of an epoch, of a country, of an idea...

It is true it is said that we design. But it is because there is no other word, and because this one is established. It is agreed. As for us, to be accurate, one could say that we draw objects for some people. Sometimes furniture sometimes spaces, sometimes technical objects, sometimes everything at the same time. So, design doesn't mean much here. For a long time, design meant drawing a product for everybody. Today, it rather means drawing all kind of products for one person.

Matali Crasset

As for me, I do industrial design, that is to say I conceive objects the nature of which is to be industrially produced. In addition, I sometimes practice scenography or interior architecture, but I don't mix disciplines, I make allowances.

I prefer being a designer than an industrial aesthetician. I think that being a designer, even if what this implies is not really asserted, it is clear that it doesn't mean only dealing with the shell of things.

Designer... I think that in people's mind, a designer is the one who puts little thingumajigs on a shape to make objects distinguishable. Have a look in the catalogues, in the magazines, the 'design' object is always the one with the unneeded thing, a touch of colour, a detail, a superficial 'gimmick'* that distinguishes it from the others. I'm afraid by the idea that this is the way people are explained what design is, a mere fancy!! As for me, in my native village, they don't know what a designer is, so I'm labelled 'artist'.

Nowadays, design has become a digestive profession. In the past, it was the profession of hyper-productivity, of excessive consummation, of equipment, of development etc. We have everything now. We have the capacity of doing everything, so what can we do? We must thus digest, define a frame inside of which we can do things. We must think about how we can do better, use better, understand better too. Digest!

Jean-Marie Massaud

Design... it has become a trendy word, it's hype now, design. But for the others, it's more of a style. In fact, in both cases, it doesn't suit me. Design means more of a state of mind to me, before being a practice. It is a way of looking at our environment and unceasingly questioning ourselves, sometimes even unconsciously, on the situation and the way to improve it. And all this before even having touched a pencil. This is the reason why I generally find all definitions a bit reductive.

Design is conceiving an object in which we will project our vision of the ideal environment. Each object we draw has a part of its own, an intrinsic quality and a symbolical quality, that is to related to the image of the world we offer. Design, architecture, scenography, I don't want to see any difference

*(in English in the original)

Je suis bien quand je suis allongé sur le sol

Cosmic Thing, 1997
wool, steel, wood
Carte blanche VIA
Design: Patrick Jouin
Ph: VIA

Fluxus, 1998
aluminium, wood
Carte blanche VIA
Design: Patrick Jouin
Ph: VIA

Facto, 1997
steel
Ed: Fermob
Design: Patrick Jouin
Ph: VIA

between these disciplines, in the sense that each project has a double value. By designing a chair, I think I also define a bit of architecture.

A designer is the one that at the end proposes alternatives in terms of either life styles or life qualities. Drawing the objects is something that comes last. The proof is that innovation today is not to be found anymore in the one button that will involve the activation of something special in a machine, but in the will to see how this machine allows or proposes another solution in its relationship with the user. The invention doesn't lie in the object anymore, but in its interaction with the environment.

One can sum this up by saying that, before, a designer was the one who would make an object in one given system, today he is the one who questions a system and proposes a more sensible alternative to it.

There is also another interesting idea about our practise today. A designer is someone who has a phenomenal quantity of creative material at his disposal. Be it technological, formal, ergonomical, cultural, what else… a whole nebula of existing material. Creating today that's also drawing on this material, the ingredients, the elements that we will gather together in a particular manner and giving this combination a new value. Creating, that's not only inventing, the way an engineer invents something that wasn't existing before, that's also organising already existing things, composing, to provide a new service, a new performance, a new sense.

Pleasure

Matali Crasset

I don't design for my own pleasure. I mean that pleasure is not the first motivation of my work. Pleasure comes as soon as you have established communication, when you see that your project is correctly read, when the one person, or the persons to whom you are speaking have understood what you wanted to say. In fact, when something is shared.

Jean-Marie Massaud

Pleasure is my motivation. Work is above all making things that won't make me sad. And then, I have a big fault: I'm lazy. It is not that I am affected, it is a real pain for me to get to work. So what matters is the pleasure I will find in working. I pay particular attention to make my work look like something else than labour. By permanently changing the field of my intervention, a house today, tomorrow a perfume bottle, you always discover new things, you don't have the impression to practice a profession, with all the routine it may imply. That's what I have discovered and what I like in design.

Patrick Jouin

I design for my own pleasure. It's basically very personal. It's my means of expression. I only inject it in the society afterwards, so that it can play a role, be useful.

Mathilde Brétillot, Frédérique Valette

As far as we're concerned, we draw things we like, or things that represent a world in which we would like to live, that's all. We enjoy drawing. It is first the expression of our sensibility, of our desires. We don't have any precise aim, any precise destination. There is not necessarily any strong stylistic unity in our production. The images of these objects vary according to our moods, our experiences.

Committed

Matali Crasset

In the past, commitments were sharper. They revealed a true reaction, a true opposition to an idea, an established system. In the sixties and seventies, grand utopias urged people to be radical. Today, the commitment is more discrete, more homeopathic. The conflict exists inside a system, not outside of it. I also think that though it is less visible, it engenders a real evolution. We've immersed ourselves in the system, because we've chosen to make it evolve from the inside, with the means it offers: industry, production, economy, communication.

Maybe it is a less monolithic commitment. It is carried out in the cracks.

I've been taught a profession that consists in making objects, so I do my best to design these objects, so that they can, one by one, form a brick in the building of an evolution.

Patrick Jouin

What drives me is a communist approach. I mean a generous and certainly altruist approach. Following the example of the Art and Craft movement in which the idea of giving, sharing and improving is essential. My commitment is a social commitment, but it is not restricted, identified as a mission. It is more vague, like everything is today; tastes, desires, aspirations have all become eclectic.

What comes out of the nineties, is the withdrawal of political commitment. It is a more cynical generation that doesn't believe in revolution anymore. It is a more mature and less naive generation. Today, thinking of wiping the slate clean, thinking in terms of revolution would be very naive. Things can improve in a constructive way, without anything to be broken. But then what is being done is less visible, more discrete, more humble. Before, designers were socially and ideologically commited: Branzi, Mari. They contested the system and objected grand utopic principles. Today, we belong to the market, to the capital and to the production context. We don't fight this context, we use it.

The objects we draw today are more discrete. They are more 'affectuous'. 'Discrete friends'. They don't tell less, they simply do it more slowly. It's like homeopathy. They diffuse rather than they speak. Hence the necessity for mass production.

Jean-Marie Massaud

My commitment is not far from my pleasure. I don't see myself as being a troublemaker, but I don't think it is unacceptable to commit oneself to produce pleasure, mystery, magic, to imagine worlds, let's say rather environments, more sensual, more peaceful, happier environment. I never saw myself as a prophet, I don't consider myself to be very rebellious, but I believe it is legitimate to be able to give that point of view. If committing quality is to be defined, I would say I am the counterweight. I hate conformists and I believe a part of my work is used for showing that when one thing seems to be acquired, another, a different one, can be as valuable, if not better.

Mathilde Brétillot, Frédérique Valette

Everything is being produced today, everything exists, one thing and the exact opposite. I think it is necessary to find references. People, I mean we, need references to distinguish or discern things in a system that would be close to the magma. Making, again and again, is not necessary. Things must be thought of, objects, furniture, products, that are truly addressed to people, that would have a real and sincere emotional link with them. If not, it is space filling, and there are enough objects here.

Style

Jean-Marie Massaud

I love doing work that is 'obvious'. I didn't say 'archetypes', I said 'obvious'. I'm looking to design things that aren't necessarily obvious to the first degree, but that stand out by their simplicity, their density, and their logic. I wouldn't go so far as to reduce the form of an object to a logo, but I would wish for it to be a simple symbol. My long-chair for example, is an ideogram of rest: a base, and over it a flexible line that says 'relaxation', that's all. I'm not looking to add feet, arm-rests or ornaments.

Matali Crasset

Forms don't really fit in my field of research. Of course I create forms but they are merely the result of an intention. They will crystalise or materialise an idea. There are so few cases where I say to myself that I'll change the form of an object. That's not how I function, and I don't think I'm good at that. That's not where my role comes in.

Beef

Once again, we're not trying to define ourselves. True, we have our personal tastes, our own methods, but that doesn't define a style. We act differently according to our clients requests. I think our work is based on simplicity and on the emphasis of minute details that produce a distinct difference. We use for example, very often the same lettering, which is a standard lettering on which we spent a lot of time working on the space between the letters. It might seem a bit derisory, but for the reader the difference is huge. We also pay very close attention to colour. We're working now with Japanese colour charts, that aren't very common, but where the colours quality, richness, and intelligence of selection have nothing to do with ordinary traditional colour charts. Although we work most certainly on the infinitesimal and on detail, we have as an objective to affirm a bold difference.

Mathilde Brétillot, Frédérique Valette

We're not looking for formal heroism, we design humble but malicious things, the originality of which is found in a surprise or rather, a subtlety. The objects we design are usualy very simple, nearly obvious, however, we spent an enormous amount of time attaining the form. I'm under the impression that we design objects by their contour, in a very graphic manner, very refined. Although we obviously think of our object as being three dimensional, it's more by a figure that their shape is found. This idea of the figure shows us how to correctly see the objects. In one motif, all the essentials are said, so it is all immediately understood. This allows a richness of material, colour, a substance that isn't ornamentation or unneeded extras.

French

Matali Crasset

It's a bit complex. Before, there were schools where people grouped or were grouped together by their stylistic similitudes. It turns out that these schools are usually associated with geographic locations, countries. Today, it's a bit more complicated but we try nevertheless to 'store' people, even if it's not very legitimate, just because it must be reassuring to put simple generalities and obvious guardianship to control better, to therefore understand better. I find it more interesting to see that today there are very similar steps in Europe and if we are to gather certain people, it would be fairer to do so with the particularity or the similitude in the process. Proto-Design in Portugal, Oliver Wogh and Weiseneger in Germany, those are examples of people that should be put in relation, regardless of their origins. The rest doesn't make much sense. It's not so much my roots, which could have given me a singularity at work, I think it's more of my 'villageoise' backgrounds. For example when I collaborated with Denis Santachiara, we noticed that we were very alike. He too came from a small village, in Italy. I think that this personality, driving from our origins, is much stronger and affective than the fact of being French or Italian.

On the other hand, I believe that there are effectively common cultural features between peoples of the same country. But this can be found in all professions without us having to define it as being a school. We don't say 'The Accounting School of Germany' or 'The Real-Estate Promoters of Italy'. Sure, culture is present in our actions, but does that make me a French designer?

The interest I see in being a French designer nowadays, is that there is so little, that there is so much to do. On the other hand, in Italy, there are so many people and so many things, that it doesn't leave much perspective.

Beef

Being French or being English is a question we don't ask ourselves. French? If we were to ask ourselves, we would say it is a 'qualification' we prefer not to endorse. France is a very poorly cultivated if not, not cultivated at all, country in terms of graphic design. Look at what is being done is the world today and compare it to the logos and images of big French companies. You can't say that they really seem concerned with graphic design. Take for instance the logo of the soccer world cup. Ridiculous. Everyone found it ridiculous, but, well, they did it anyway. Somebody decided it could be done.

I find graphic design in France so minor. It is always seen as being in a predetermined conventional domain. In England, on the contrary, there is always this expectation and desire to 'extend' their limits. We relate much more to that.

Jean-Marie Massaud

My behaviour and personality are much more Latin than Nordic. I love living and my work reflects that. But it does not make me a French pure product. Furthermore I think that what we mean today by French style or French specificity is more of in a folklore order than reality. Many countries share with us what is considered to be French. I would say I'm French lack of

Goodnight, 1997
steel, 2 60w bulbs and coton
Design: Patrick Jouin
Ed: VIA

Ph: PJ

anything better, or as an actual fact. For example, I'm fascinated by Japanese culture, but I'm so far away from being able to be part of it. Furthermore I don't see French design. Where's 'the' French design? Is it Liaigre? Is it Starck? Is it Garouste and Bonetti? I see no French in my work even if it is my cultural background.

Mathilde Brétillot, Frédérique Valette

Design is becoming more and more international and has a tendency to create a scene that's becoming more and more levelled. What interests me here, is to remember that one of the motors of creation and the creator's sensibility, is his singularity which will produce the originality of his work. If someone is to ask us French, to draw something, it's that they have been previously seduced by a certain quality. I find it pertinent in this sense to ask ourselves about our nature and therefore on our French particularity. Our culture, our mind, our reason, our sensibility. It's not to characterise, but maybe just to have consciousness of a form of quality that is not shared by the whole world.

Global

Matali Crasset

It is true we are called upon to intervene in numerous different practices, architecture, scenography, fashion… Yet, I don't have the feeling I intervene globally. I think I intervene in each discipline with my nature to design, my practice to design, and my view to design. That's what I find interesting. The fact that we are not intervening globally, but that we approach disciplines with a methodology, taking different steps to those that are common, or standard to each practice. I think this difference, this singularity is what the people are looking for when they call upon us for these projects. I recently made a bar without even taking in account the space. The whole functioning and behaviours induced in the space relate to the objects and furniture that I design. I think an interior design can only reason that way.

I like the idea of keeping this professional particularity, a specialised skill that allows a special angle of things. Or else I really don't see much interest for everyone to do everything.

Beef

The global dimension, or universal dimension of all creative work is merely the logical consequence of the will to gather the largest number of persons around an idea. It's not bad. The question today is the speed of the phenomenon. Take techno music, a few years ago, it was a very avant-garde music, very elitist, and very contested. It only took a few months for it to become universal and for us to hear it in about every commercial. There is now a cult, a hysterical one, over the 'new'. It only takes something to be new for it immediately to become a model gathering people, then it's no longer new, so they all pass to the new news!

Jean-Marie Massaud

By global I mean world-wide. Globalisation has sometimes had the purpose to give access to certain things that were not accessible and that wouldn't have been accessible without globalisation. But this is often impoverishing. I'm all for singularity. Not regionalism, singularity. I find interesting the idea to create things that can be shared universally without them being the product of a reductive levelling. For example, certain Japanese cars have been made to fit a certain category of people. There is globalisation, there is also singularity. The difficulty is that one must address an individual and not a mass. One must find in a product a sufficient amount of abstraction allowing appropriation by all. The idea is a bit complex but it's what I'm looking for. For instance, in my new perfume bottle, it doesn't mean creating common places or insignificant objects. It might mean finding different levels of lecture in objects addressing people in a more sensible manner, less cultural. I think that's what should be worked on, and not to advocate a return to the local or regional, that will in the worst case give the effect of folklore. Folklore is like globalisation, folklore is the same everywhere.

Mathilde Brétillot, Frédérique Valette

Globalisation leads to a loss of identity, or rather a loss of identity as they meant in the past: local originalities. Behind that, what bothers me is the loss of curiosity. When everything becomes similar, I feel that we are no longer urged to see, to search, to know and understand. What feeds curiosity is difference. Design mustn't lead to that, or else we'll all end up living in international airports or Holiday Inns.

◀ 1

▼ 2

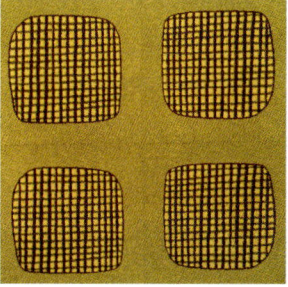

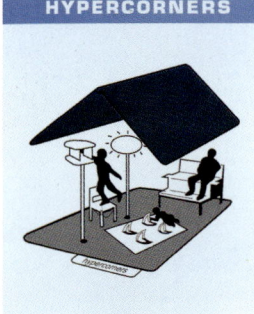

HYPERCORNERS

LISADOUBLELIFE

NANO-ARCHITECTURES

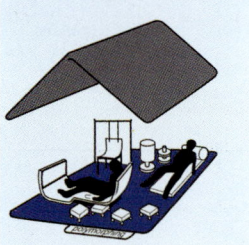

POLYMORPHING

◀10

◀11

◀12

13 ▶

14 ▼

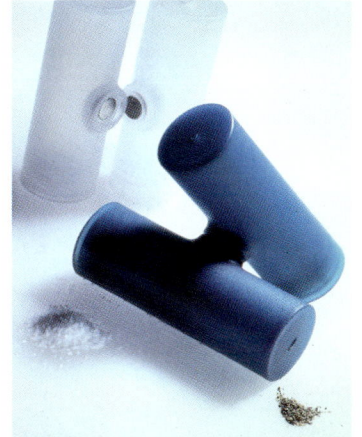

◀ 15

◀ 16

17 ▶

18 ▼ 19 ▶

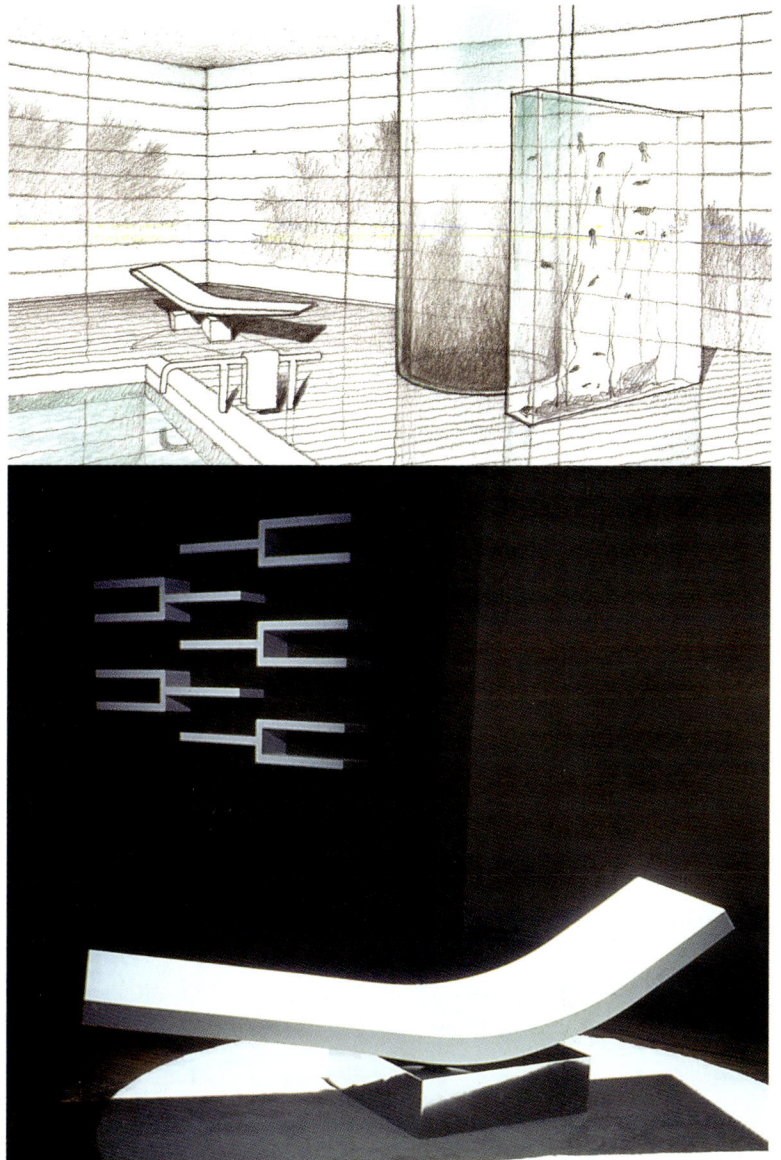

22 ►

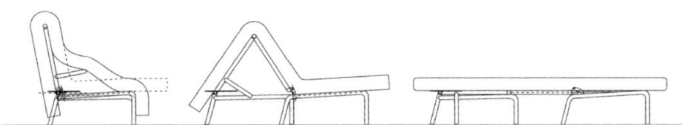

23 ▲ 24 ►

25 ►

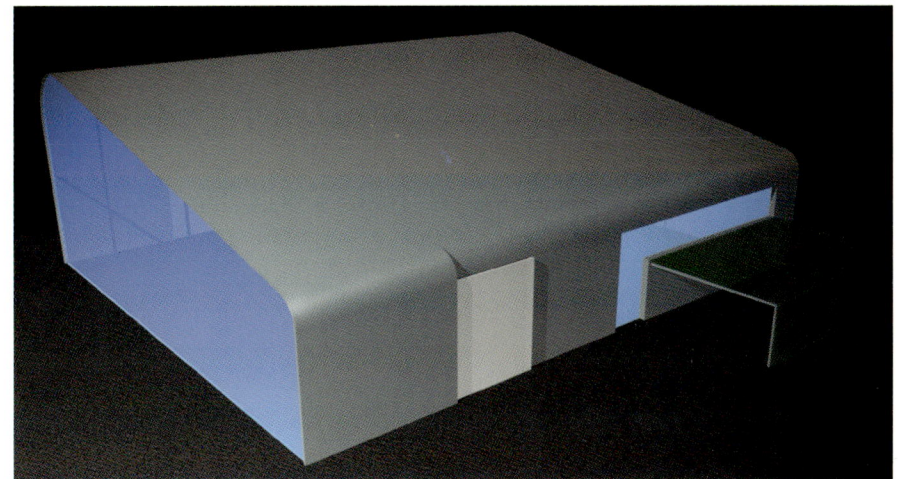

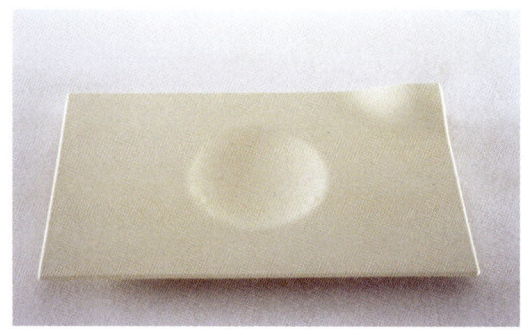

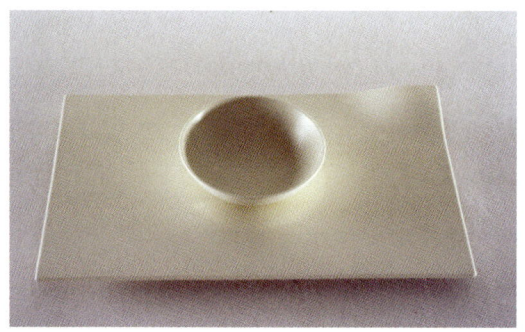

31 ▶ 32 ▶

33 ▶ 34 ▶

35 ▶ 36 ▶

◀ 37

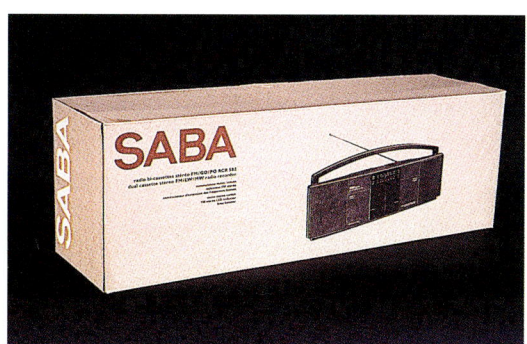

◀ 38 ▲ 39

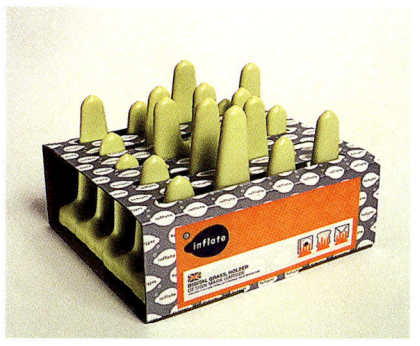

◀ 40

41 ▶

42 ▶

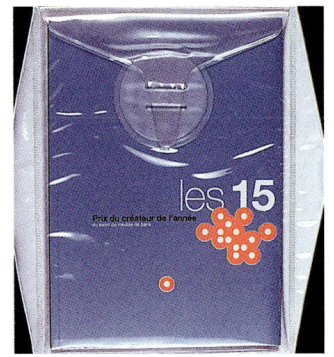

Color Photographs Index

1: *Icaro*, armchair, 1994
stainless steel base and cloth
Design: Brétillot/Valette
Ed: Driade, Italy
Ph: Mario Pignata

2: *Cryptée*, textile tile TESCOM, 1999
polyamid
Design: Brétillot/Valette
Ed: SOMMER France
Ph: Christophe Fillioux

3: *Excelsior*, dish, 1997
hand decorated porcelain and guilded metal
Design: Brétillot/Valette
Ed: La Manufacture de Sèvres, France
Ph: La Manufacture de Sèvres

4: *Sans Titre*, lamp project, 1998
blown glass and aluminium
Design: Brétillot/Valette
Michele de Lucchi Private Collection, Italy
Image infographique

5: Hypercorners
Design: Matali Crasset

6: Lisadoublelife
Design: Matali Crasset

7: Nano Architectures
Design: Matali Crasset

8: Polymorphing
Design: Matali Crasset

9: *Empathic Chair*, with its extension *Home for a Child*, system of urban modular furniture, 1996
recycled plastic and metallic structure
Design: Matali Crasset
Young designer Grant, Sandberg Institute, Amsterdam
Collection Fonds National d'Art Contemporain
Ph: Nicolas Profit

10: *Icipari*, portable alarm-radio
ABS plastic and gum
Design: Matali Crasset
Artistic direction: Philippe Starck
Ed & Ph: Lexon/Thomson, 1995/1999

11: *Quand Jim monte à Paris*, hospitality column, 1998
wood, nylon, coton, hight ductility foam
Design: Matali Crasset
"les amis de matali" collection
Ed: Domeau & Pérès, La Garenne Colombes
Ph: Morgane Le Gall

12: Exhibition design by Matali Crasset for the forum "laine et lin"
"Première Vision" Fair, 11/14 March 1999
Ph: Vincent Leroux

13: *Cono Vision ou Bicolor*, magic glass, 1998
polypropylen
Design: Matali Crasset
Ed: Authentics, Holzgerlingen
Ph: Markus Richter

14: *Place mat n°4*, set of table mats, 1998
polypropylen and silkscreen printing
Design: Matali Crasset
Ed: Authentics, Holzgerlingen
Ph: Markus Richter

15: *Tohot*, salt cellar, 1998
propylen + magnet
Design: Jean-Marie Massaud
Ed/Authentics, Germany

16: *Hot*, pepper mill, 1999
polypropylen, stainless steel and ceramics
Design: Jean-Marie Massaud
Ed: Authentics, Germany

17: *O'Azar*, chairs 1998
air moulded polypropylen and beach wood
Design: Jean-Marie Massaud
Ed: Magis, Italy

18/19: *Lola,* stacking column chair
air moulded polypropylen + aluminium
Design: Jean-Marie Massaud
Ph: Studio Massaud

20: *Tanabe,* house (section), 1998, ongoing project
Design: Jean-Marie Massaud

21: *Horizontal Chair*, 1999
technopolymer with protein and stainless
Design: Jean-Marie Massaud
Ed: E & Y
Ph: Mario Pignata Monti

22/24: *Morphée*, 1998
steel, foam, cloth and wood
Design: Patrick Jouin
Ed: Ligne Roset
Ph: VIA

23: *Krazy Jacquet*, 1995
cloth, stereo speaker, tape player
Design: Patrick Jouin
Ed: SABA et Adidas
Ph: Thomson

25: *Don O*, portable radio-tape player, 1995
ABS plastic
Design: Patrick Jouin, Matali Crasset
Direction artistique: Philippe Starck
Ed & Ph: Thompson Multimédia

26: *Al*, shelves, 1999
extruded aluminium and laser cut art plywood
Design: Patrick Jouin
Ed: Proto Design
Ph: Computer-generated image

27: *Factory* pour 2000
steel, concrete and Virginia creeper
Design: Patrick Jouin
Ed: Plastique
Ph: PJ

28: *Wave,* 1999
earthenware
Design: Patrick Jouin
Ed: Gien Earthenware Manufactur for Alain Ducasse
Ph: Nicolas Profit

29: *Luxlab* (installation, Milan Fair), 1999
mutable ground: pressed aluminium structure,
lawn mattress (fongicidal protection)
fireplace: stainless steel, Pyrex glass
liquid table: glass top + water
Design: Jean-Marie Massaud, Patrick Jouin, Thierry Gauguin
Ph: DEIS

30: *Super mini,* 1998
aluminium and lawn
Design: Patrick Jouin
Ed: Mobile
Ph: Laurence Hazout

31: Corporate identity for Basenotic Records Paris, house techno label, 1997
Design: Beef

32: Corporate identity for Janvier, post production house, 1999
Design: Beef

33: Vinyl bagde for Basenotic Records, 1997
Design: Beef

34: Corporate identity for Inflate, London, 1996
Design: Beef

35: Exhibition Catalogue for Jasper Morrison, Marc Newson and Michael Young in Iceland, 1999
Design: Beef

36: "Repères 99", catalogue for the Paris Furniture Fair, 1999
Design: Beef

37: Television packaging for Thomson, 1997
Design: Beef

38: Audio packaging for Thomson, 1996
Design: Beef

39: Audio packaging for Saba, 1996
Design: Beef

40: Packaging for Inflate, London, 1998
Design: Beef

41: "Air Garden", invitation for Tom Dixon and Inflate, Japan, 1997
Design: Beef

42: "Prix du créateur de l'année", catalogue, Paris, 1998
Design: Beef

Beef

Biography

Simon Clark, born in 1972 in Edinburgh and Sébastien Dragon, born in 1970 in Le Havre, met by chance within of a large French consumer electronics company whislt collaborating with Philippe Starck in 1995.

Beef, as it's known was born two years later, a natural progression, working from a fixed base in Paris with an essential mix of varied clients. The desire to communicate and create new ideas began with a common understanding and passion for graphic design. The enthusiasm which drives Beef has accelerated them into many other areas of design.

Beef are continually evolving... and now have a department working on 3 dimensional projetcs and are expanding further and opening an office in London at the begining of september 1999.

Their main clients are:

Biotherme–BNO Record–Dupont Lycra–EC One London–Expofil, Galeries Lafayette –Inflate London–Janvier– Lanvin–L'Oréal Paris–Pillet, Christophe–Saba–Salomon–Salon de Meuble–Sainsbury's–Sonneti–Starck, Philippe–Telefunken–Thomson–What's up Record

Graphic Design

1995

Design with Philpe Starck for Thomson Multimedia for the world electronics exhibition, Berlin included: extensive product graphic development, logotypes, exhibition graphics, 7m x 4m framed light box image....
Corporate brochure design for Thomson Multimédia
Connections magazine for Thomson Multimédia
Corporate identity for product design group Inflate, London
Logotype for Tim Thom, Studio 2 P. Starck
Audio packaging for Saba, conception and implementation graphic guide (for approx 100 products a year)
Headed note papers for Thomson, Telefunken, and Saba
Logotype "deus" international standard satellite

1996

Art direction for BNO records, Paris
Art direction for BPM records, Paris
Series of headed note papers, packaging, brochure design, advertising and product graphics, for Inflate, London
Audio packaging for Thomson, conception and implementation graphic guide (for approx 250 products a year)
Radio packaging "poe" for Alessi, Italy
Logotype "digipro" with Philippe Starck for Telefunken
Product catalogue for SABA
Web site menu pages creation for Thomson Multimédia
Exhibition design for Philippe Starck, Edifice, Paris

1997

Corporate identity and all stationary for Otonet, Belfort, France
Television packaging for Thomson, conception and implementation graphic guide

Video tape recorder packaging for Thomson, conception and implementation graphic guide
Winter 1998 Prediction Book (limited edition) for "Expofil" and Jannette Hack at View on Textiles
Corporate identity, shop front and all stationery for Ec One, London
Concept development for a new chain, "Fnac junior",France, stationery, packaging, sign systems; etc.
Annual report 1996, Thomson Multimédia
Sainsbury's supermarket chain, UK (on going project)
Limited edition book for Paris Furniture Fair 1998
Logotype "Electronic Program Guide" for Grundig, Phillips and Thomson
Professional shampoo packaging range "Osmose", 60 products range, for L'Oréal Professionnel, Paris
Range of trend books for Lycra

1998

Paris Furniture Fair, exhibited a new range of shower curtains *Shampoo*
L'Oréal Professionnel Paris, professional hair colour packaging range "Majirel"
L'Oréal Professionnel Paris, professional haircare packaging range for men including product and graphic development
L'Oréal Professionnel Paris, professional perm kit packaging range
SABA consumer electronics catalogue 1998-1999
Galeries Lafayette, Paris, exhibition graphics "wedding trade show"
Inflate book "swell" published by form magazine

Intervention at the Reims University level college for Art and Design
Packaging & catalogue for the "Thomson collection line"
Corporate identity for What's up record, Paris

1999

Range of snow boards for Salomon
Catalogue "Repères", for the Paris Furniture Fair
L'Oréal Professionnel Paris, merchandising and product development
Lanvin, perfume packaging
Saba consumer electronics catalogue
Corporate identity of Janvier, Paris
Catalogue for Jasper Morrison, Mark Newson and Michael Young, Iceland
Art direction and design for men Fall-Winter catalogue Sonneti, England
Biotherm packaging development
Inflate product catalogue

Brétillot/Valette

Biography

Frédérique Valette, born in 1959 in Lyon, graduated at the Ecole Camondo in 1984, collaborated with P. Starck from 1984 to 1994.

Mathilde Brétillot, born in 1959 in Paris, graduated at the Ecole Camondo in 1984, collaborated with Mr. Bedin in Milan from 1984 in 1987, with R. Lovegrove in London in 1987, with P. Starck from 1991 to 1994.

At school (Camondo) together, personnalities and several countries enriched their professionnal experiences. In 1991 they joined Philippe Starck. In 1994, they decided to share their projects. And in 1997, they gave concrete expression to the image of their duo setting up the studio Brétillot Valette Interior Design.

Consulting et teaching:

Pedagogic coordination since 1994 for the department of Design of l'ESAD, the Superior School for Art and Design in Reims. Art direction for Techniques Transparentes, G. Saalburg S.A since 1996.

Interior architecture:

Mistic, restaurant in Tokyo, 1986 (P. Starck)
Manin, restaurant Manin in Tokyo, 1987 (P. Starck)
Royalton, Hostel in New York, 1988 (P. Starck).
Paramount, Hostel in New York, 1990 (P. Starck)
Hugo Boss shop in Paris, 1991 (P. Starck)
Placido Arango, private house in Madrid, 1992 (P. Starck)
Felix at The Peninsula, restaurant in Hong Kong, 1994 (P. Starck)
Museum in Groningen, Netherland, 1994 (P. Starck)
Ecole des Arts Decoratifs in Paris, 1993 (P. Starck)
Laguiole shops in Paris and Toulouse, 1991 and 1995
Yannick Morisot - Photograph agent in Paris, offices, 1991
Artists residence, the Arques, South of France, 1994
La Coface, exhibition design for the Porte Maillot Fair in Paris, 1995 & 1996
Atlantic Codental, offices and show room in Paris (1995)
Fred, competition for the fixing-up of the shops in Cannes, France, 1996
C. Vernes, offices, bank, Paris, 1997
Private house in Paris
Top Cloud, restaurant, for The Shilla in Séoul, South Corea (ongoing project)
Exhibition design of "De Main de Maître" (ongoing project, 1999-2000)

Furniture & Object Design

Solid - Co-founder member, Milan, Italy, 1986
Bags for J & F Martell, France, 1987 & 1989
Mixer taps for Jacob Delafon, France, 1988 (M. Bedin)
Flos- Miss SISSI, Italy, 1990 (P. Starck)
Bubu, stacking stool, Les Trois Suisses, France, 1990 (P. Starck)
Ashtrays, La Seita, France, 1991
Urban Furniture, Decaux, France, 1990 & 1992 (P. Starck)
Handbags and luggages for Esprit, USA, 1992 (M. Bedin)

Chair, *Sintesi - Gironde*, Italy, 1995
Icaro, armchair, Driade, Italy, 1995
Urban Sign - Malakoff, France, 1995
Vases, Manufacture de Sèvres, France, 1996
Perfumes, launching of GIO for men, for Armani, 1996
Fastening accessories for bags, for Coach, USA, 1997 (for R. Lovegrove)
Carpet tile Tescom, Sommer
Lamps, La Collezione Privata
Furniture, Collection Tropicale, Ile de la Réunion (ongoing project)
Office accessories for Mace
Un jeu d'enfant, for the association Escarlopettes in the mission for the year 2000 celebration

Exhibitions:
"Solid" in Milan and Paris, 1987 & 1989
"Neolite" in Milan and at the Seibu Art Forum in Tokyo, 1989 & 1991
"SAD 90", Grand Palais, Paris, 1990
"Novator 91" in Troyes, France, 1991
"Les maîtres de demain" at the Seibu Art Forum in Tokyo, 1992
"Richesse et Pauvreté, (exhibition of unique pieces)", off Furniture Fair of Paris, 1997
"Justine 'tit' chaise", Paris, 1998
Stand and exhibited products G. Saalburg, Furniture Fair, 1998
Stand and exhibited products, Opaque Diffusion, House and Objects Fair, Villepinte, 1998
Soirée Nomade, 18th June 1998 at the Cartier Fondation: vases
Exhibition design of "Sommertime", Off Furniture Fair, 1999

Bibliography
Solid, Electa Editions, 1986

Matali Crasset

Biography

Matali Crasset was born in 1965 in Châlons-en-Champagne. Graduated in design at the E.N.S.C.I. in 1991, she took part in the Triennial of Milan, where she exhibited her project "la trilogie domestique". She worked then with Denis Santachiara in Milan on architecture, design and exhibition projects. Back in Paris in 1993, she collaborated during five years with the studio of Philippe Starck. From 1994 to 1997, she was also responsible for the Multimedia Thomson project then for the Tim Thom, design center of Thomson Multimédia. She set up in 1998 her own structure in Paris. In 1999, she won the Grand Prix de la Presse Internationale de la Critique du Meule Contemporain for *Quand Jim monte à Paris* edited by Domeau & Pérès.

Furniture & Object Design

1993

Eb'brezza, vase, for Domodinamica, Italy

1994

Quality award, trophy, for Thomson Multimédia, Paris

Rotondino, egg cup-saltcellar in porcelain, for Rosenthal, Selb-Bayern

O + O, walkman, for Saba, Thomson Multimédia group, Paris

Range of TV set (*Saba M 5107, Saba T6308, Saba T6349 SL, Saba T 7008, Saba T 7049 SL*) *Ibid.*

1995

Don-O, portable radio-tape recorder, for Thomson/Telefunken, Paris

Range of TV set (*Palcolor S4400 stereo, Palcolor S4400 hifi-stereo, Palcolor S4400 sat-stereo, Palcolor S5400 hifi-stereo, Palcolor S5400 stereo, Palcolor S5400 sat-stereo, Palcolor FS 533 stereo, Palcolor FS 533 stereo*) for Telefunken, Paris

TV Rack 100, TV set and video-tape recorder unit, *Ibid.*

Space system SC 81PL, stereo & color TV set 16/6 81cm, for Thomson/Normende, Paris

Space system SC 60, TV set color & stereo 16/6 60cm, *Ibid.*

1996

Aloo, cordless phone with digital answering machine, for Thomson, Paris

1997

Zahnbürstenbecher-Toothbrush cup, toothbrush pot in polypropylen, for Authentics, Holzgerlingen

Don-O, portable radio-tape recorder, for Thomson, Paris

1998

Bicolor, magic glass in polypropylen, for Authentics, Holzgerlingen

Bath set, vertical soapdish in polypropylen, *Ibid.*

Place mat n°4, set of table mates in silkscreen printed polypropylen, *Ibid.*

Quand Jim monte à Paris, "hospitality column", for Domeau & Pérès, La-Garenne-Colombes

Il capriccio di Ugo, armchair with tablet-armrest, for Domodinamica, Italy

1999

Icipari, radio-alarm in ABS and gum, for Lexon, Argenteuil

Téo de 2 à 3, stool and nap bed, for Domeau & Pérès, La-Garenne-Colombes

Marcel kangourou, "Marcel", silkscreen, printed T-shirt, for Nekt, Paris

Pet's tray, pets' food dish in polypropylen, for Authentics, Holzgerlingen

Bird's house, bird cage in polypropylen, Ibid.

Light for h, lamp, (ongoing project) *Ibid.*

IN/OUT, soft key case in silicon, (on going project), *Ibid.*

Icon's shower, shower curtain, silkscreen printed, (ongoing project) Ibid.

Home wax, candle with double-mèches, (ongoing project) Ibid.

Daily starting bloc, shoe brush, for Die imani-gäre Manufaktur, Berlin (ongoing project)

Me-You, ring for two in silver, for S.M.A.K., Reykjavik, (on going project)

Prototypes (selection)

1991

Trilogie domestique, light, heat and water diffusers

1992

Xandrin, stool to read fairy tales

Anamnesico, anamnesic miror

Bozzolo, furniture for children to take a nap with metal structure/F.I.T.

Hard and soft W, hi-fi tidying furniture

1995

Cub, domestic diffuser of images, projector retroprojector LCD, dream product Thomson Multimédia

Perso, confidential, portable, face to face visiophone dream product Telefunken

1996

The empathic chair, urban furniture concept realised with the support of Sandberg Instituut, grant "Young designer Grant"

W at hôm, domestic office furniture in the context of la carte blanche du V.I.A.

1997

Jules est plutôt dandy, chair with peg

1998

Glassex projects:

- *Oritapi*, carpet for children 2D/3D
- *Prince magique*, table-stool
- *Casadrome*, seats/resting structure
- 3 pièces, desk
- *Francis shoes*, travel shoes with unique sole
- *In case of*, multi-fonction pants
- *Bat-chair*, chair parasite
- *Human E.Pad*, computer furniture, with Olivier Peyricot

Research

Collaboration with l'A.N.A.T. and Frédérique Lamaignère for the settings of a composite F.I.T., Thermoplastic Impregnated Fiber, and metal for a furniture auto-portable structure

Intérior architecture/exhibition design (selection)

1988

Area, stand design for Saga in the Grand Palais, Paris

1989

Maison des Arts de Créteil, design of the bar and the bookshop

1993

Thomson Multimedia, design of the exhibition for the show of tv sets "Jim Nature" & "Oz" by Philippe Starck in Paris, Madrid, Munich and Milan

1997

Intramuros, scenography of the exhibition "Paris/Milano: rencontre avec la nouvelle génération" in the Ara di Diogène - Milan
Liturgical furniture for the Chapelle de la Maison de Marie, Fondation Sue Ryder, Lourdes

1998

Exhibition design for the Who's Next Fair

1999

Intramuros, exhibition design with Claire Escalon, "Desseins de Femmes"
Exhibition design of the Who's Next Fair
Musée des Arts Décoratifs, marocan café inside the exhibition "L'objet désorienté au Maroc"
Première Vision, exhibition of the forums "laine et lin", exhibition design of the "sportwear forums, denim and activewear"
Realisation of the interior architecture of an appartment (ongoing project)

Collective exhibition (selection)

1992

Milan, XVIIIème Triennial of Milan

1993

Paris, Furniture Fair, V.I.A.
Londres, I.C.E., "Design & Metamorphosis"
Milan, Fondation Mudima, "12 designers per incatare l'atmosfera"
Paris, Centre Technique du Bois et de l'Ameublement, "Materiaux d'avenir"

1994

Paris Furniture Fair
Amsterdam, Stedelijk Museum, "Young industrial designers 1994: Holland - Germany - France"

1995

Cologne, Banhof Deutz, "Waterlily European Award under 35"
Berlin, Internationale Funk Austellung, "Thomson Multimédia: dream products"
Paris, Carroussel du Louvre, "Design: art ou industrie?"
Paris, Furniture Fair, V.I.A. (the House of the Five Senses) and La Métropole (Domestic Plastics)
Paris, Centre National Georges Pompidou, Atelier des enfants "Les portes du design ou l'aventure de l'objet"

1997

Paris Furniture Fair, V.I.A. "homo domus - variation sur le confort de l'homme"
Milan, Ara di Diogene, "Paris/Milano: rencontre avec la nouvelle génération"

1998

Milan, International Furniture Fair, Domodinamica
Paris, Colette, "matali in colette" with Michael Anastasiades

1999

Paris, Glassbox, "Glassex", exhibition designed with Olivier Peyricot and Lisa White with Olivier Peyricot, Xavier & Izumi Moulins
Paris Furniture Fair, "Women in Design"
Hambourg, stilwerk Design Center, "Objet de charme: neues Design aus Frankreich"
Turin, Palazzo Cesare Alfieri di Sostegno, "Big Torino 2000: international biennial of young creation"

Solo exhibitions

1998
Berlin, modus

Bibliography (selection)

Books
Thierry de Beaumont, *Dictionnaire International des Arts Appliqués et du Design* (dir. Arlette Barre Desponds), Ed. du Regard, Paris, 1996
Design 10 ans: les actes du colloque, (with the retranscription of the conference of Matali Crasset), E.N.S.A. of Nancy, 1998

Essays
Jardin des Modes, N°160, 1992, Paris
Intramuros N°51, 1993, Paris
Jardin des Modes, N°186, 1995, Paris
Etapes Graphiques, N°6, 1995, Paris
Eurofocus, N°7, 1995, Paris
L'Evènement du Jeudi, N°590, 1996, Paris
Design Fax N°79, 1996, Paris
Jardin des Modes, N°193, 1996, Paris
Beaux-Arts Magazine, N°154, 1997, Paris
Design Report, March 1997, Hambourg
Beaux Arts Magazine, N°155, 1997, Paris
L'architecture d'aujourd'hui, N°310, 1997, Paris
Design report, N°8, August 1997, Hambourg
Marie Claire Maison, N°335, September 1997
Marie Claire Maison, N°341, May/June 1998, Paris
Design Net, N°9, June 1998, Seoul
Interni, N°482, July/August 1998, Milan
Elle, N°2748, September 1998, Paris
Barfout!, special issue "Paris is burning!", automn 1998, Tokyo
Mobile, N°1, December 1998, Paris
Interior View, N°13, January 1999, Paris
Blueprint, N°158, February 1999, Londres
Crash, N°7, May 1999, Paris
Le Monde, 3th of July, 1999, Paris

Patrick Jouin

Biography

Patrick Jouin was born in 1966. Graduated from the ENSCI in 1992, he began working for Wagons Lits, then, from 1993, he joined Philippe Starck's Tim Thom for Thomson, where he participated in the conception and development of a varied audiovisual "dream" products. Since 1995, he has been working in the studio of Philippe Starck where he is primarily devoted to furniture and industrial design. In 1996, he received from the VIA an "appel pemanent" that enables him to deal with a new technology: malleable wood. On a personnal basis, he has designed furniture for Fermob, Proto Design, Resistube, Ligne Roset, and Ducasse). Carte Blanche of VIA (1997), he was for the first time exhibited in the Milan Furniture Fair in 1998. Since may 1999, he has been an independant designer.

Furniture & Object Design

Dolby Surround Boos Speakers, DAP Starck, edited by Thomson Multimedia, September 1995

Téléviseur 55" stereo, DAP Starck, edited by Saba, September 1995

Don-O stereo, radio-tape recorder, DAP Starck, édited by Thomson Multimedia, September 1995

Morphée, bed-sofa, edited by Ligne Roset, January 1999

Chair and table *Facto*, edited by Fermob, January 1998

Al, shelves, edited by Proto Design, April 1999

Service *Wave* for Alain Ducasse, earthen-ware factory of Gien, June 1999

His main clients are: Fermob, Proto Design, Ligne Roset, Ducasse, Thomson

Prototypes

"Appel permanent" from VIA, Furniture Fair of Paris 1997: chair Facto, bed Good Night, Lamp Light Watt

Carte blanche from VIA, Paris Furniture Fair 1997: Bed-sofa *Morphée*, table-carpet *Cosmic Thing*, screen-lamp *Wonder Wall*, trestles *Fluxus*

Solo exhibition:

Salone Satellite, Milan 1998

Group exhibitions:

Paris Furniture Fair 1997, stand VIA

Milan Furniture Fair 1997, stand VIA

Paris-Milano, Intramuros, Milan 1997

Paris Furniture Fair 1998, stand VIA

Cologne Furniture Fair 1998, VIA

Label of the VIA, Paris 1999

Paris Furniture Fair, Ligne Roset

"Des Corps Mobiles", Carroussel du Louvre, 1999

VIA Label, Paris 1999

Salone satellite, *Luxlab*, Milan 1999

Bibliography

Les Villages 1998: Terminologie et pataquès, ed Hazan, 1998

Les Villages 1999: Confort et inconfort, ed Hazan, 1999

Jean-Marie Massaud

Biography

Jean-Marie Massaud was born in Toulouse, France, in 1966. Graduated in 1990 at the ENSCI - Ecole Nationale Supérieure de Création Industrielle, he worked with several design companies in Asia and in France until 1994, where he set up his own design studio in Paris. He then devoted himself to industrial design and furniture design, dealing with European or Japanese companies such as Authentics, Baccarat, E & Y, Magis and Yamaha. He developed also architecture projects, supported by Japanese partners. He currently holds a teacher position at the Ecole Nationale Supérieure des Arts Décoratifs de Paris, where he gives lectures with a contextual approach orientated to a research of the Essential, where the indidual stays in the center. A quest of meaning, of magic, and of vital emotion.

His work, for which he won numerous prizes, has been included in the permanent collections of main design museums in Amsterdam, Chicago, London, Paris and Zurich.

Furniture & Object Design

Furniture and lights with few English, French, Italian, and Japanese companies.

Varied products, art of table, perfume, clothes and accessories, office furniture and accessories, for German, French, Italian and Japanese compagnies.

His Main clients are: Authentics - Baccarat - Back - Cacharel - Cambrai Chrome - Comet - Domeau & Peres - E & Y - Golden Whale - Habitat - ICM - Lancôme - Lanvin - Lexon - Magis- Mazzega - Mizuno - Nekt - Technal - Yamaha offshore

Interior architecture/exhibition design

Tanabe, house, Japan

Architecture concept for the shops of a luxury trade mark

Department store Cleaning, Tokyo, Japan

His main clients are: Ecole Centrale Nantes - MGTB. Ayer - Magis - Ville de Ramatuelle - Ville de Lyon - Cleaning .

Solo exhibitions:

VIA "carte blanche", Paris, 1996

"Horizontal", E & Y-Tokyo, 1998

"Think horizontal", Musée des Arts Décoratifs, Paris, 1999

Group exhibitions

"Paris Milano", Milan, 1996

"Made in France", George Pompidou Center, Paris, 1997

"La vie en rose", Cartier Fondation, Paris, 1998

"Forma Italia", Chicago Athenaeum, Museum of Architecture and Design, 1998

"Des corps mobiles", Carrousel du Louvre, Paris, 1999

Bibliography

Monstra del 17° Premio Compasso d'Oro, Silvia Editor 1995

50 lights, Rotovision Editor, 1997

50 products, Rotovision Editor, 1998

Monstra del 18° Premio Compasso d'Oro, Silvia Editor 1998

Also available from Dis Voir

CINEMA

Jean-Pierre Rehm, Olivier Joyard,
Danièle Rivière
Tsaï Ming-liang

Jean-Marc Lalanne, Ackbar Abbas,
David Martinez, Jimmy Ngai
Wong Kar-wai

Paul Virilio, Carole Desbarats,
Jacinto Lageira, Danièle Rivière
Atom Egoyan

Michael Nyman, Daniel Caux,
Michel Field, Florence de Mèredieu,
Philippe Pilard
Peter Greenaway

Christine Buci-Glucksmann,
Fabrice Revault d'Allonnes
Raúl Ruiz

Yann Lardeau, Jacques Parsi,
Philippe Tancelin
Manoel de Oliveira

CHOREOGRAPHY

Paul Virilio, René Thom,
Laurence Louppe, Jean-Noël Laurenti,
Valérie Preston-Dunlop
*Traces of Dance–Drawings and
Notations of Choreographers*

ARCHITECTURE

Christian de Portzamparc
Genealogy of forms

DESIGN

Pascale Cassagnau, Christophe Pillet
Starck's Kids?
*(Beef, Matali Crasset,
Jean-Marie Massaud,
Patrick Jouin, Brétillot/Valette)*

Chloé Braunstein, Gilles de Bure
Roger Tallon

Charles-Arthur Boyer, Federica Zanco
Jasper Morrison

Pierre Staudenmeyer, Nadia Croquet,
Laurent Le Bon
Garouste et Bonetti

Philippe Louguet, Dagmar Sedlickà
Borek Sìpek

Raymond Guidot, Olivier Boissière
Ron Arad

François Burkhardt, Cristina Morozzi
Andrea Branzi

ÉDITIONS DIS VOIR
3, RUE BEAUTREILLIS—F-75004 PARIS
PHONE (33/1) 48 87 07 09
FAX (33/1) 48 87 07 14
EMAIL: DISVOIR@AOL.COM